"Mom Loved You Best"

Viking

"Mom Loved You Best"

WILLIAM E. HAPWORTH, M.D.

MADA HAPWORTH, M.A., M.A., PSY.D.

JOAN RATTNER HEILMAN

To Wills—

You are so wonderful that we did not want another child to cloud our love and loyalties.

VIKING
Published by the Penguin Group
Penguin Books USA Inc., 375 Hudson Street,
New York, New York 10014, U.S.A.
Penguin Books Ltd, 27 Wrights Lane,
London W8 5TZ, England
Penguin Books Australia Ltd, Ringwood,
Victoria, Australia
Penguin Books Canada Ltd, 10 Alcorn Avenue,
Toronto, Ontario, Canada M4V 3B2
Penguin Books (N.Z.) Ltd, 182–190 Wairau Road,
Auckland 10, New Zealand

Penguin Books Ltd, Registered Offices:
Harmondsworth, Middlesex, England

First published in 1993 by Viking Penguin,
a division of Penguin Books USA Inc.

10 9 8 7 6 5 4 3 2 1

Copyright © William E. Hapworth, Mada Hapworth,
and Joan Rattner Heilman, 1993
All rights reserved

Portions of this book first appeared in *Men's Health* and *Redbook*.

LIBRARY OF CONGRESS CATALOGING IN PUBLICATION DATA
Hapworth, William.
"Mom loved you best" / William and Mada Hapworth with Joan Rattner Heilman.
p. cm.
ISBN 0–670–83756–3
1. Sibling rivalry. Brothers and sisters. I. Hapworth, Mada. II. Heilman, Joan
Rattner. III. Title
BF723.S43H34 1993
155.9′24—dc20   93–6898

Printed in the United States of America
Set in Postscript Caslon 540
Designed by Kathryn Parise

Preface

Many people have passed through our offices at the Hapworth Centers, the medical and psychiatric facility that we founded almost a decade ago in New York. We and our staff have had the privilege of experiencing our patients' lives in a way that few others are ever permitted. Most of us get only a glimpse of other people's inner selves after they have been edited for general consumption. But, as professional psychoanalysts, we have viewed these lives unadorned, as they really are. Our patients have entrusted us with the raw material, allowing us to see the parts of themselves they consider most secret, most unattractive, most in need of repair.

In our clinical work, we have become aware of the importance of siblings, along of course with parents, in shaping personalities and affecting one's views of the world. We have learned how profoundly brothers and sisters cast their shadows on one another, how their every social interaction, every emotional response to another human being, is irrevocably affected by their relationship with their siblings. Yet, strangely, that relationship has always appeared to be the black hole of psychotherapy.

Most of psychoanalytical theory is obsessed with the Oedipal Complex as the key to the development of who we are and the unique styles we use in getting through life. Until now, there has been little interest in what we call the "Sibling Complex," the powerful connection between brothers and sisters. Although Alfred Adler, who along with Sigmund Freud and Carl Jung is one of the three founding fathers of psychoanalysis, pointed out the significance of the sibling relationship, it has been only in the last few years that its importance has been acknowledged among professionals and its true implications seriously studied.

The views we express in this book are a compilation of thirty years of our collective experience with our patients whom we see once or twice a week in individual, family, or group therapy. They have provided us with incredibly rich case histories. As we delved into every minute part of their psychological beings, we came to understand their insecurities, courage, failures, and successes. To protect their privacy, however, we have carefully disguised their stories, not only by changing their names but by altering and merging their experiences. We hope that we have not breached their trust in any way.

In addition to our therapeutic experience, we have both had extensive psychiatric and psychological training that culminated in internships/residencies at New York University Medical Center and Bellevue Hospital in New York, where we met. We have also both had the rare opportunity to be trained and analyzed by the children of Alfred Adler.

It is the Adlerian belief that the guiding force for humankind is the desire for mastery and superiority in our efforts to control our universe. We have seen that it is in the sibling relationship where the first awakening of these universal human strivings often occurs. We use this philosophy in our efforts to understand our patients and make sense of their worlds.

You are not alone in wanting to understand the complex connection between you and your siblings. It is confusing and frustrating to find yourself again and again repeating the same dysfunctional and unsatisfying behaviors, never realizing why you did them or why you can't stop. It is our belief that by examining the sibling relationship you will be unburdened from its inevitable conflicts and rivalry and empowered to live a happier, healthier, and freer life.

—Bill and Mada Hapworth
New York, 1993

Acknowledgments

Our thanks to:

The experts—our patients—who have trusted us with their cherished secrets;

Our friends and colleagues, who have patiently tolerated our long absences and accepted us back when we found the time;

Our editor, Mindy Werner, and our writer, Joan Rattner Heilman, who, despite the wars we went through, stood their course and brought the book home;

Our agent, Janet Wilkens Manus, who had faith in us from day one;

Our parents and siblings, who helped make us who we are today and gave us the emotional material to draw from. Especially to Tina—for her courage to work through sibling issues with us, so we can enjoy our lives together;

Millie, who was always available to help out in any way, with encouragement and love;

And most of all, to Wills, who never fails to fill our lives with wonderment and love.

Contents

Contents

"Mom Loved You Best"

Close Ties: The Power of
The Sibling Connection

If you have ever wondered why you get along famously with one of your siblings, are always ready to hang up the phone on another, and feel like going to bed for three days after talking to a third, this book is for you. It is designed to help you understand the enormous power of the bond between you and your siblings and the enduring rivalry that is the essence of every sibling relationship.

As you explore this powerful relationship, you will find invaluable clues to your own behavior, clues that may have eluded you all of your life as you have tried to understand yourself. You will finally have some answers to why you do what you do and how you turned out to be who you are.

In the process, you will become much better able to understand, tolerate, and perhaps even greatly improve your relationship with your brother or sister. Only when you have sorted out the patterns of behavior, subtle or obvious, that you and your sibling use on one another, can you see how they came about. And why, despite the passage of time, they never seem to change.

Perhaps the most important thing we hope you will learn is that *all* brothers and sisters spend their lives in competition with one another. They are rivals, whether they realize it or not. This is as true for siblings who are close and supportive as it is for those who say, "I'd never choose her for a friend. If she weren't my sister, I'd never see her again!"

Sibling rivalry is the fuel that fires the relationship between brothers and sisters. It never disappears even after you have all grown up and gone your separate ways. All adults, carrying with them powerful feelings left over from their childhoods, remain eternally locked in a power struggle with their siblings—especially one of them—in an everlasting contest for control and supremacy. And the resentment and jealousy, buried or acknowledged, benign or bitter, that they harbored toward one another as children stands ever ready to be reactivated, often when they least expect it.

Just as power is an important ingredient of all human relationships, it is an inescapable part of the sibling connection. The issue is who is going to end up with more or less of it. In our own unique ways, we all try to get as much power for ourselves as we possibly can. Why? Because each of us desperately needs to feel competent, accepted, adequate, worthy, and—most important of all—in control of our environments. We want to feel we measure up, that we are winners. Even more, we cannot bear to feel like losers (except when there's something in it for us).

Power is more than merely the ability to control other people, making them do things they may not want to do. It also includes the ability to protect ourselves by predicting and anticipating the behavior of others. And, in this case, it encompasses the certainty that our brother or sister will always be there, part of our history and our lives, forever.

In our power struggle, our siblings turn into measuring rods for our own worthiness. Always comparing ourselves to them, sometimes consciously, sometimes not, we conduct continuous evaluations. Are they doing better or worse than we are? Who is the more worthy person? Who has the best job, who makes the most money, who's married the superior mate, whose children are the most successful, who has more friends, a better character, more prestige?

This doesn't mean we are always at odds with a sibling, constantly struggling for superiority and control. Only when we feel personally exposed, vulnerable, or challenged do those unwelcome rivalrous feelings rise unbidden to the surface, triggering the same old self-protective responses we learned back then when we were young. This is the way it is for everyone who has ever had a sibling, although some of us suffer from it more than others.

That's why sibling relationships can *never* be perfect and why they are *never* exactly what you'd like them to be. There's hardly a person on earth who doesn't have complaints, major or minor, about a brother or a sister and disappointments about the interaction with them. By their very nature, *all* sibling relationships are dysfunctional—at least in some ways and at some times—between even the closest of siblings. Furthermore, the discomfort is always reciprocal. You can be sure that if you are experiencing pain or disappointment in your relationship, so is your sibling, however reluctant he may be to admit it.

Take, for example, Sally Ann, the intelligent, energetic 53-year-old assistant principal of a suburban junior high school. Satisfactorily married and with four grown children, she says her older sister Marian is her best friend. "We would do anything for one another," she says. "We talk at least twice a week and I know she'd always be there for me."

She hesitates and then adds, "But I can't be around her too much. She always makes me feel I'm not measuring up—like, why don't I organize my kitchen better or how come I don't get out to see Mom more often. She's a perfectionist. Her home is spotless, exquisitely decorated, she dresses beautifully with the shoes matching the bag and earrings coordinating with the pin.

That's fine but I can't relax around her because she's always criticizing, sometimes just with a certain look that I know so well.
How do I handle it? I don't say anything because it's not worth
fighting over, but sometimes I could kill her. Do I retaliate? Sure,
in my own cowardly way. I know all her weak points, like her
hangup about getting old. So when I'm really fired up, I sneak in
a couple of remarks about wrinkles or gray hair. Or I don't call her
at our usual hour on Saturday mornings. I make her pursue me.

"It's not something you think about because it's all so childish.
You just do it and realize later what you've done. Sometimes you
never even know you've done it until someone points it out to
you. Then you try to rationalize it away, or justify it, or pretend
you didn't really behave just like you did when you were little
kids."

In her efforts to feel adequate and worthy, Sally Ann's sister
placed great value on her own organizational abilities and felt
compelled to imply that Sally Ann's were inferior. Sally Ann, in
turn, countered by feeling she was a much better person than
Marian because she kept the peace and did not dispense guilt
trips. Furthermore, she regained a sense of control by making her
big sister run after her.

Life Is Not Fair

Every family has its inequities, and the allocation of the parental
prizes of love, acceptance, attention, and approval never comes
out exactly even. Even if it did, deep down we probably couldn't
perceive it that way. All of us grow up feeling the other got more
of something than we did. All of us feel inferior, at least in some
ways at some times, to a brother or a sister. Because of that, all of
us harbor resentments toward the other that can remain a potent
ingredient of the relationship if we live to be 103, although the intensity varies and the way in which it manifests itself is a matter
of style.

Because most of us were raised to believe we must unconditionally love our brothers and sisters, these people whom we had no part in choosing, we feel guilty and bad about ourselves when we don't. We want brothers or sisters who are nothing short of wonderful, always on our side, and we are desperately disappointed when they don't come up to our expectations. But the truth is that it is impossible to feel unadulterated love at all times for someone who is trying to control you and assert superiority over you. And that is the job of a sibling.

Feelings of resentment, envy, jealousy, fear, deprivation, hurt, rejection, embarrassment, guilt, rage, ambivalence, and a variety of other "unacceptable" emotions toward these people who are inextricably tied to us for life are not only natural but universal. Sibling rivalry is simply a fact of life. You can deny it and suppress it, you can understand it and accept it, you can change it and improve it, but you can't get rid of it.

The Big Blind Spot

A troubled sibling relationship is among the most common problems adults face. And yet it is probably the least discussed. We have found that when our patients talk about their lives in the course of psychotherapy, they almost invariably minimize, even negate, the influence of their brothers and sisters, considering them merely unimportant witnesses or accomplices. Rarely are they aware that their siblings have been powerful forces in their lives.

In our culture, sibling relationships are not considered important. Our bonds with parents—and later with spouses, lovers, and children—are thought to be the only profound connections we make. Few of us realize that the bond between brothers and sisters is the *other* significant relationship in our lives and that the Sibling Complex—the constellation of all the effects of this relationship, and the way its jealousies and resentments are resolved—is the *other* most important factor in determining our ultimate personalities.

Perhaps it's because brothers and sisters have always been so much a part of the scene that we fail to pay much conscious attention to them. Maybe, in our egocentrism and desire to be in control of our own destinies, we are reluctant to acknowledge that anyone except our parents could have had such an important impact on the way we turned out. It is not easy to admit, "My sister or my brother made me what I am today." Who wants to give them so much credit?

Or perhaps we deny the importance of siblings because of their tremendous potency. The purpose of denial, a well-recognized psychological maneuver, is to disguise our most sensitive issues. Frequently the more emphatic the denial, the more emotionally charged the issue. In working with our patients, we have found that those who refuse to acknowledge problems with siblings sometimes have the most insidious and destructive relationships of all because they have allowed their unresolved conflicts to affect them profoundly without realizing it.

Shaped by Our Siblings

Along with environmental and parental influences and genetically determined characteristics, the sibling relationship is responsible for the development of our personality, our perceptions of the world, and our roles in it. Obviously, the overwhelming part that parents play in shaping us can't be denied. Our parents formed the essence of our character, identity, values, moral codes, goals, defenses, and techniques we use to cope with life. But parents are only one very important part of the equation. The second most essential ingredient is our sibling relationship.

Because parents are authority figures and not peers, we cannot compete with them directly. They have too much of a head start, too much power and control for a fair fight, and the stakes are too high to risk defying them openly. Besides, parents are bound by different rules than children, and society places different expectations on them. They issue commands from on high, while their children scramble to maneuver around their dictums. Parents tell us what to do. Siblings force us to figure out how to do it.

That's why our brothers and sisters, more or less our size, more or less our equals, teach us more than our parents ever could about making our way through life. They give us our first lessons in competition, showing us how to get along, constructively or neurotically, with other people. The sibling "laboratory," where we test new feelings and behaviors, allows for countless experiments in socialization, providing plenty of time and space to analyze the results of our actions and make the necessary adjustments. Siblings are our models, showing us how to play together, work together, fight together. They form our first alliances and our first betrayals. They are living examples of behaviors that work or don't work as we compete with them for power, love, attention, and the approval of our parents.

By the time we have grown up and left home, each of us has constructed a personal template, a permanent pattern for social interaction that has been molded by our experiences within the family.

The Power of the Familiar

You, like everyone else, leave home carrying with you the conviction that everything will always be just like it was back there. Your family has set the pattern for how you will behave in all of your future relationships.

And what's wrong with that? Nothing, if the behaviors you learned are functional in the outside world. But problems arise when the tactics and techniques that were so successful at home don't elicit the responses you have come to expect. Does that mean you're going to change your ways? Probably not. Even when your customary behavior does not work out to your advantage, you are not likely to change it, because it is much more comfortable to stay just the way you are. Once you have been conditioned to respond in a certain manner, it is extremely difficult to extinguish that learned response, especially without the intervention of psychotherapy, a strong mentor, or a powerful and/or traumatic experience. Challenged or threatened, you, like all of us, tend to revert to your same old patterns, the ones you learned when you were growing up.

The influence of your siblings permeates every aspect of your adult life, from how you make decisions, get along at work with superiors and peers, deal with friends, neighbors, admirers, and enemies, and even how you choose and treat your spouse and raise your children. Your brother(s) or sister(s) shaped you so effectively and indelibly that there is little you can ever do that is not dominated on some level by your relationship with them.

It is their ability to preordain what feels familiar and therefore comfortable to you that gives siblings their greatest and most enduring power over you. In this vast world, the options are infinite. But you will navigate your course everywhere you go guided by your own personal radar system that is programmed to seek out the familiar. Dealing with people and situations you "recognize," however unknowingly, provides a sense of security and control, so you go through life with a tendency to turn everyone you meet into a reincarnation of those you left behind. You will always be attracted to people who resemble your real siblings, whether you were close friends, ardent adversaries, or, more likely, a combination of both. And even when the resemblance isn't all that close, you will *see* other people as your siblings and so you will involuntarily respond to them as you have always responded to the originals. Most of the time we aren't even aware that we are doing it. And when it is pointed out that we are recreating the familiar, we wonder how we could have been so blind not to see it at the time.

•

Take Regina, who appeared in our offices for her first therapy session in hysterics. Between gasps, tissues, and tears, she related that she had not made the cut for director at the investment bank where she was employed as a stock analyst. She didn't understand it. She had had straight "A's" in business school. She was a good and conscientious worker, keeping long hours, doing a thorough job, getting along well with her bosses. This was the third time in ten years, however, that she had been passed over.

With our help, Regina eventually realized that she'd never made the grade because of the behavior she had learned at home to deal with the competition. The youngest of four children, the only girl, she had a father who was a defense attorney for big-time mobsters. She worshiped him but always felt he took her three older brothers far more seriously than her. She learned very young that the only way she could gain a feeling of superiority over her brothers was by undermining them. When she reported their misbehaviors to her father, who was determined his boys would not turn out like the criminals he represented, the results for them were devastating.

As an adult, Regina continued to use the same self-enhancing technique. When she felt threatened, she pointed out her competitors' bad judgment, recounted their errors, and had even gone so far as to examine one colleague's electronic mail and keep notes on his indiscretions. However, her tactics were not appreciated by her superiors. Just the reverse, such tactics earned her nothing but distrust and disfavor because her employers were looking for team players.

It took Regina a long time to recognize the behavior pattern that worked against her own best interests. Now that she has, you'd think it would be easy for her to change her style. But it isn't. Like an addict who keeps returning to her stash, she feels compelled to snoop and tattle on her rivals whenever she feels insecure. But she is beginning to understand the self-destructive behavior she learned to use with her brothers and that it won't work outside of the family.

The Powerful Sibling Bond

Not only are you eternally influenced by your sibling relationships, but you will always be bound to your brothers and sisters by amazingly strong ties. Siblings give you something you can get no-where else. They are your most intimate and most enduring rel-atives, irrevocably tied to you by history and commonality. You may not have spoken a word to your brother in twenty-five years or you may quarrel with your sister at least once a week. You may consider your sibling your closest friend, sharing your innermost thoughts, or you may feel she is no longer relevant to your life. But close at hand or continents away, love them or hate them, even dead or alive, siblings are part of the inner landscape of your experience. They will be very important people to you until the day you die. Even in the least connected or most contentious of relationships, you can disengage or write them off, but you can never erase them from your head for good. While it is possible to drop friends and acquaintances and even serious romantic attach-ments from your life with little emotional residue when circum-stances and feelings change, you can't drop siblings. They, like your parents, are part of you and yours forever.

Tying you together is the intimate knowledge you have of one another. No matter where you have gone or what you have done, there is no one who can possibly know you as well in so many subtle ways as your sibling. Your brother or sister knew you long before you developed the almost inpenetrable protective coating of social veneer and the clever disguises that come with adult-hood, long before you met your spouse, had your children, en-countered your friends. He or she has shared the important core experiences of your early life. That's why there is no one who knows your secrets—the small unspoken fears, the desires, ambi-tions, shame, the vulnerabilities you carefully hide from others—better than the brother or sister who grew up with you. And no one who knows better how to use this secret information to help you or hurt you. Your sibling retains the lifelong ability to "push your buttons."

•

One day in a group therapy session, Rebecca told the story of her eldest daughter's wedding when she happily introduced her younger sister Ruth, present for the occasion from across the continent, to all of her guests. Her delight in having her sister there soon turned into dismay and embarrassment. Seated together at the same table with Rebecca's two daughters, the sisters began reminiscing about their early family life. Enjoying it at first, Rebecca soon began to feel uneasy as her daughters listened to tales of her childhood through her sister's eyes and she found herself portrayed as bossy and critical. Just as she had when they were small, Rebecca felt Ruth was trying to make her look bad and to come between her and those she loved. To make matters even worse, her younger daughter heartily agreed with her aunt that Mom was indeed bossy and critical. Rebecca felt betrayed. Ruth, in return for the ever-painful feeling that Rebecca had been their mother's favorite, had indeed pushed her buttons.

•

Along with that intimate knowledge of one another, siblings tend to share a form of shorthand. Although you may have very different personalities or may be separated by many years, you and your brothers or sisters tend to speak a common language and share common symbols. You have learned a special tongue that only family members can fully understand. Because of shared experiences, you reference the same events. You access the same information from the same cues. You have the same inner code of ethics—the set of values every family holds in great esteem—whether you live by it or not. It's doubtful you will ever have another relationship where there is such rapid transfer of knowledge and feeling, or such insight into the inner workings of another person. Brothers and sisters can often telegraph thoughts and feelings with a glance, a gesture, a couple of code words, even when they haven't been together for years.

Another powerful link is your common memory. Siblings are the historians who chronicle your past. They can corroborate or rebut, confirm or refute your perceptions of epic events and minor incidents because they shared them with you or watched them happen. No one but a brother or sister can verify your memories and fill in the gaps so well, although their recollections may not always be identical to your own. Grownup brothers and sisters inevitably reminisce when they are together, comparing perceptions of the past. Was Dad really a success in his business? Did Aunt Sally hate Uncle Willie or did it only seem that way? Remember the silence at the dinner table after that terrible fight? Wasn't it fun when John came home with the baby squirrel? How about the time you hit me with the baseball bat?

Even a sibling who is many years older can confirm your impressions and verify your recollections. It's difficult to fully explore on your own what it meant to grow up in your family. Siblings have information you are seeking because they were there.

"My sister and I feel tremendous bonding because only we two knew what went on in that house," said one of our patients in group therapy. "Only we two can remember the way our mother made my sister out to be the bad one and recall the snide comments about every boy Jill ever dated. We're the only people in the world who can talk about that. We're the only ones, too, who know about Dad's beatings, Mom's complicity, and the fact that our parents weren't the pillars of society everyone thought they were."

The Ten Commandments of Siblinghood

Sibling relationships have been a subject of fascination since history began. Parents as far back as Adam and Eve saw the potentially powerful forces between brothers and sisters. Mythical tales as well as biblical references have always drawn attention to the love and conflict between them. Always, groups that considered themselves bonded have called themselves "brothers" or "sisters," and political leaders have used the terms to express solidarity and power for their preferred concepts and movements.

Perhaps because of the powerful feelings siblings have for one another, the relationship between siblings since the beginning of humankind, has depended on an unwritten set of commandments that draws the boundaries of acceptable and unacceptable behavior. These rules encompass the values, norms, and mores that most of our Western societies consider essential, handed down through the generations, acting as the cement that keeps families together. When these rules are broken, the family as well as society metes out justice ranging from discriminatory treatment to disinheritance and/or exclusion.

We have all grown up drawing on this large legacy of ideas, especially in the Bible, that has evolved into an approved code of behavior, limiting and controlling the interactions of siblings. We refer to them as the Ten Commandments of Siblinghood. Although many of them are broken all the time, they provide guidelines that keep the institution functioning and help us determine our sense of self-worth and whether we are good or bad people.

- *"Once a sibling, always a sibling,"* is the first Commandment. No matter what you do, where you go, or what you become, you are a brother or a sister. Throughout history and legend, siblings have performed the most dastardly deeds against one another but the relationship has endured.

- *"You are your brother's keeper"* is Commandment Two. This means you must take responsibility for your sibling, despite his follies, misbehavior, or betrayals, and come to his aid when he needs you. The story of Cain and Abel illustrates this commandment. Cain, the older brother, jealous because God preferred Abel's offerings to his, rid himself of his rival by killing him in the field. When the Lord asked what became of Abel, Cain responded, "Am I my brother's keeper?" God answered in the affirmative, then punished him by exiling him and tainting him with the "Mark of Cain" for eternity.

- *"Rivalry is acceptable—up to a point,"* says Commandment Three. You may be competitive but not merciless. In the well-known Bible story, Jacob disguised himself as his older brother, Esau, and so was given the blessing their near-blind father meant to bestow upon Esau. This wrongfully gave him the inheritance and the power reserved for the eldest son. Esau, resenting the treachery, considered killing Jacob and even went so far as to enlist an army to aid him. But at the moment of truth, Esau could not strike the vanquishing blow against his brother. Finally embracing and forgiving him, Esau found a way for the Lord to bless him too.

We have often seen a patient, just at the point of a triumphant victory over a sibling, step back, think again, then become protective of the loser. Whether the retreat is the result of love, the dread of abandonment, or the fear of reprisal, it is clear that siblings often revel in the rivalry and superiority they feel but cannot bring themselves to decimate their familiar competitor.

• Commandment Four demands that *"the code of silence not be breached."* All families have their secrets and all family members know implicitly from an early age that they must keep them. Sometimes these secrets are the repressed demons that scar our lives and cast a constant shadow over our actions and perceptions because divulging them can bring devastating consequences. Often the need to keep these secrets is a major obstacle to going into therapy because the idea of revealing them to outside ears implies betrayal of the family.

The code of silence is supposed to protect siblings as well as parents, and it usually does. Siblings often hesitate to reveal, for example, a brother's mental illness, a sister's shoplifting record, or an abusive relationship for fear of betraying the family image, although jealousies and resentments frequently prompt intentional hostile social exposure of a brother or sister that intensifies the conflict. But, even in a moment of intense rivalry, what is divulged seldom crosses the line into open betrayal. Instead, it is only hinted at, with an implied threat of telling all if behavior doesn't change.

• Commandment Five requires that *"siblings must accept one another."* How many times, after her sister had destroyed her favorite possessions, did Julia hear from her mother, "She's your sister, the only one you have, and you just have to take her with her good points and her bad"? This cardinal rule of siblinghood says that, no matter how we feel about them, we must not completely reject these people who were born to the same set of parents.

The ultimate testimony to turning the other cheek is told in the biblical story of Joseph and his brothers. Jealous because, as the youngest and his father's favorite, Joseph was given a beautiful coat, his brothers stole the coat and sold him as a slave. Many years later, when Joseph was a rich man but his treacherous brothers were starving, he forgave them and took care of them.

• *"Incest among siblings is taboo,"* is Commandment Six. What is supposed to be a platonic relationship between siblings sometimes becomes a sexual involvement, a subject rarely discussed in families and never considered acceptable. The Greek and Egyptian gods were no strangers to the temptations of incest, often having intercourse with their siblings and usually getting into deep trouble because of it. In the Old Testament, Abraham married his half-sister, for which he was cursed. Job's seven sons slept with their three sisters and were punished when, despite their father's atonement, great winds caused their house to collapse, killing all of them.

Incestuous relationships can obviously cause chaos within a family, disrupting the orderly chain of command that normally places the parents in charge. Sexualization can give one sibling great power over another, not only because of the resulting guilt, shame, and anger, but because of the secrecy that attends it.

• Commandment Seven is *"Nor is it acceptable to covet your brother's or sister's children or your in-laws."* Marriage brings into the family people who are not related by blood, often creating enormous sexual tension and sometimes resulting in clandestine affairs designed to undermine a sibling. Not only are these in-laws not related by blood but they have different codes of behavior and different definitions of "good" siblinghood. Bringing them into the family often creates major upheavals because, since they are not governed by the same rules, their interest does not lie in the survival of the family but of their marriage.

• According to Commandment Eight, *"You must honor your sibling but not more than you honor your parents."* In families as well as in society, the lines of authority must be clear or there will be anarchy. The survival of the group depends on the foot soldiers—in this case, the children—carrying out the orders of their superiors. So, children must give their first allegiance to their parents. The Bible is full of stories that emphasize the importance of honoring your parents above your siblings. For example, Eli's sons, wicked and greedy, rebelled against him. Eli went to the Lord to complain about their behavior and God told him He would kill his sons on that very day, and He did.

• Commandment Nine is *"You must love all of your siblings equally."* This is an easy rule to follow if you have just one sibling, but very difficult when there are more of you. Although it is impossible to love everyone the same, multi-siblings are reluctant to admit that they prefer one brother or sister over another even when it is obvious that they do. So they do their best to disguise their favoritism, much as parents do about their children.

• Finally, Commandment Ten gives power to the family unit by insisting that *"The family has the right to decide how close the sibling ties must be and what is needed to be a 'good' or a 'bad' member of the sibling group."* In some families, it is sufficient to send Christmas and birthday cards and speak to one another once every six months. In others, you are not playing your part if you don't call your brother or sister twice a day. In some families, no demands may be made, while, in others, members are expected to give all and lend all at all times.

How can you assess your own worth without knowing what is expected of you? In your own family, what are the parameters of your sibling relationship? Are you supposed to lend your brothers or sisters emotional and/or financial support? If so, how much and at what cost to yourself? Must you put your sibling's needs and happiness ahead of your own and that of your boyfriend or girlfriend, your fiancé, your spouse, your children, your boss, your friends? In each family, the boundaries of what is acceptable in the response to one's siblings are unique, but you will be bound by yours until you decide whether or not you want to abide by them.

Moving On

Brothers and sisters can cast such long shadows over us, and we over them, that we must acknowledge their profound influence if we are ever to understand ourselves, our behavior, our likes and dislikes, our aspirations, our innermost feelings. And if we want to improve our relationships with them, we must recognize that they, like us, are hostages of their past and learn to accept them as flawed human beings, just as we are.

You may be starting off this book with a history of discord between you and these people who grew up with you. Or perhaps you have a relationship that is essentially good but marred by resentments and misunderstandings. It is even conceivable that you think you have the best possible connection. But wherever you begin, our plan is for you to come away with a better feeling about it and a greater understanding of the connection. We hope you will learn to see your brothers or sisters not as enemies, obstacles, obligations, sources of pain or frustration, but as people who have been programmed by their own personal experiences, often surprisingly quite different from yours, to behave the way they do. They too are fragile human beings who are doing their best to protect their positions and vulnerable egos against perceived threats to their self-esteem. When they lash out at you, they are not doing it to crush you but, instead, to make themselves feel taller.

You don't have to love one another just because you are brothers and sisters. But for your own peace, you must make an effort to step back and examine this relationship that affects you so profoundly. Looking at the good parts of it as well as the bad, you can decide whether it's possible to accept your brother or sister as a real friend or a source of support if only with a limited scope. If rapprochement and friendship are not in the realm of possibility, perhaps you will be able to accept your siblings for who they are, empathizing with their problems, gaining an understanding of why they are the way they are, and allowing yourself to shed much of the burden of resentment.

But, whether you improve your relationship with them or not, your explorations into this powerful connection will help you clear up many of the mysteries that have always puzzled you about yourself and your behavior.

Because rivalry is at the core of every sibling relationship, we are going to explore that first. Then we'll discuss the major influences—birth order, labels, family roles, parental attitudes—that have affected the way you feel about a brother or a sister and caused each of you to develop your own personalized techniques of self-protection. After explaining how your siblings affect the way you behave wherever you go, from the workplace to the bedroom, we will tell you what we have learned about maintaining good sibling relationships and mending those broken ties with your brother or sister.

2

The Roots of Rivalry:
"Mom Always Loved You Best!"

If you've got siblings, you've got rivals. You've got competitors who may be 20, 50, or 75 years old, but they will never stop trying to outdo you as they vie for supremacy. They may love you dearly and stand ready to lend a hand, but they will always strive to come out looking better than you. They always want to be the one Mommy loved best, the child Daddy admired most, the fair-haired boy or girl. And so do you. That's because it is the ultimate nature of humankind to strive for superiority and control in the universal search for security and acceptance.

Sibling rivalry is the desire to surpass your brothers and sisters or to maintain your dominance over them. You may compete on the tennis court or at school, on the telephone or at the dinner table, or you may compete in the safety of your mind, but whatever the arena, you will compete for first place.

"That's not true in *my* family!" you may protest. "My sister (or brother) and I have no problems. We're not competitive with each other. We get along beautifully." To that, we reply, "Look a little closer." When you do, you will be sure to find glimmers of your need to surpass and control your sibling and, at the same time, to *avoid* being surpassed and controlled by him. You may be genuinely happy and proud that your sister has won first honors in math, is marrying the most desirable man in town, or has been accepted by the country club, but there will always be at least a twinge of envy or jealousy and a feeling of inadequacy, unless more or better has happened to you too. Why? Because, at that moment, you feel you are not measuring up.

Sibling rivalry, so obvious in childhood but often deeply buried in our psyches in adulthood, doesn't fade away and disappear when kids grow up, even if we rationalize, suppress, or disavow it. We never completely outgrow it, although the way we act it out gets transformed into more subtle and socially acceptable behavior than scratching or biting to see who gets to sit on Mommy's lap. But that doesn't mean the tension of the competition, based on what we felt was our relative standing within the family as a child, has vanished. Even when there is little contact between siblings, and even when a sibling is no longer alive, the resentments can rage on inside our heads.

As children, the strictures of the family, age, intellectual development, available resources, and experience drastically limit our choices and options. We make decisions that are logical for that time and place, and our choices of winning techniques become thoroughly ingrained in our unconscious. The problem is that these programmed responses, evolved from our early struggles with our siblings, become dysfunctional when we carry them into adult life without examining their usefulness now. They may not serve us well in adulthood because they are not influenced by the new capabilities and resources we acquire as we grow older.

.

Take the case of Craig, whose rivalry with his brother, Evan, could hardly be called subtle. The youngest of three children, Craig was obsessed with overcoming his sense of inferiority to Evan. He had an older sister too, but she wasn't considered a major competitor because she was a girl and, in this family, girls just didn't count.

A grown man now, Craig could not understand why he never was able to beat Evan at any sport. He'd manage to get an impressive lead in a tennis match and then he'd choke, start missing the lines, and inevitably lose. In school, he would get the best marks in the class during the semester, but on the finals, he'd get no better than a "C." Over the years, he'd always felt the lesser of the two when their father bragged about Evan's prowess in sports and school, and he desperately wanted to prove that he was just as good, or even better.

Craig, five years younger than Evan, accepted defeat when they were kids because he was much smaller and weaker, but when they finally were close to the same size, he became determined to overtake him. "It was the strangest thing," he has said, "no matter how much I practiced and how good I got, I was never good enough." Not only that, but he began to realize that he felt exceedingly anxious whenever he was faced with competition from any quarter, always expecting to fail.

Judy, Craig's fiancée, noticed the pattern of behavior between the brothers the weekend they'd driven ten hours to Evan's home to meet him and his family and announce their engagement. Not a half hour after their arrival and an exchange of ebullient greetings and congratulations, Evan insisted on taking Craig off for a game of squash. Craig lost once more, setting the tone for the weekend.

"What's going on?" Judy wondered when, the next day, Evan took her aside to advise her not to trust Craig because he never finished anything he ever started. "He's not very responsible," he confided. "You might as well know now that he's a born loser."

It wasn't until Craig was in therapy that he began to grasp how the rivalry between him and Evan had affected every aspect of his life. At work, he competed with his superiors—and lost. He had already been fired from two jobs for insubordination. He had difficulty making and holding male friends and continued to prefer the company of women, over whom he felt superior. But he carried around in his head the fantasy that if he really wanted to win, he could beat anyone at anything, even Evan. The evidence lay in the fact that he would be in the lead all the way until the very end, loving the look of impending defeat on his opponent's face. But then he'd let the prize slip through his fingers.

He managed to acknowledge the pattern, but why could he never come out ahead of his brother (or any competitor for that matter) and, more important, why was he experiencing such anxiety when he did it? For years, he attributed it to a fear of success. Lifting the lid on his memories, he recalled their father's insistence that Evan must teach his little brother how to play sports. Dad, a top college athlete who placed great emphasis on physical ability, respected only winners, but was frugal and didn't want to pay for professional lessons for two boys.

Craig remembered when Evan taught him how to play touch football and how much he enjoyed the brutal combat. One day when he was eight, faster than his bigger but less athletically talented brother, Craig won and immediately fell victim to his brother's rage. Evan tackled him, held him down, and stuffed a handful of grass into his mouth. He threatened never to play with him again. The incident provided Craig with a powerful lesson: "Winning is losing."

Assigning Evan to the position of teacher had placed an enormous burden on both of the boys, but it carried with it an unspoken threat for Craig. He realized that beating his brother meant the lessons would stop and his father would think less of him. To prevent the exclusion, he had to stop competing or lose, so he made the best choice he could. Although he wouldn't have the total admiration his father reserved for winners, at least he would prove he was a competitor and a sportsman and, at the same time, manage to hold on to both his father and his brother. So behind the fear of success is really the fear of failure and, in this case, rejection.

But since then, a symbolic handful of grass has stood between the two brothers and prevented Craig from feeling like a winner. Through therapy, the shadow Evan cast over Craig has been brought into better perspective. These new insights have permitted

Craig to stop automatically sabotaging himself. He is no longer experiencing anxiety when he's on the brink of victory and is starting to do well in other areas of his life. He has made great progress even though his worst childhood fear has now been realized.

Two years ago, Evan picked a fight with Craig over a minor issue and has refused to speak to him since. He has, as he threatened to do years before, rejected him. Craig is very uncomfortable about the situation but he feels too positive about his increasing successes to be seriously intimidated by it. He also realizes that his father's approval is no longer so important to him. So, although he wants a loving relationship with his brother, he understands that Evan, at least for the moment, is not emotionally ready for that to happen.

Masters of the Universe

The desire for mastery and competence resides in the soul of every mortal, motivating all human development. Striving to be "all that you can be" takes us from the cradle to the grave. As babies, the struggle for mastery involves only competition with ourselves as we try to do something better than we did before. But this quickly converts from "Now I can do it better than I did before," to "Now I can do it better than *you*." That's when our mastery of self evolves into competition with others—especially with our first adversaries, our siblings.

Comparing ourselves, always judging who is in the superior or inferior position, serves a very important developmental function because it gives us a way to evaluate our own worth, define our talents, and measure our achievements and attributes. Who's the prettiest, who's the smartest, the fastest, the best, the most favored, creates a reference for life that allows us to construct a self-image and subsequently to develop self-esteem. This area in our development is most vulnerable to the effects of out-of-control rivalry and, unfortunately, always leaves one of us feeling as if we don't measure up.

•

Elsie, 37, was talking about her sister Dorothy in an individual therapy session recently.

"Dorothy is five years older than I am. I don't see her much but I'm always conscious of her and wondering what she would think of what I'm doing. She totally dominated me when we were children and I always felt she was better than me in every possible way. She did well in school, she had lots of friends, she was funny and energetic, and she obviously didn't think much of me. I was the pest who always felt left out. What gets me is that I really still feel that way today. And I think of her whenever anything important happens in my life. What would Dorothy say about it? How would she judge it? I have whole dialogues with her going on inside my head. She has tremendous power over me from hundreds of miles away. Sometimes I enjoy my accomplishments—then I think about what she would think and they suddenly don't seem so great! I made a dress from a Christian Dior pattern. I did a good job and it looked fine—but then I thought of her—and knew she would think it looked 'homemade.' "

The Plague of Favoritism

Your sibling rivalry can affect your adult life hardly at all or it can dominate your life, with conflicts ranging from small resentments to open warfare. Frequently, the parents provide the fuel that feeds the fires of resentment. As the referees in the sibling wars, they are usually ill equipped to dissipate the competition and may even believe that rivalry is needed for their children's psychological development. So they may end up inadvertently pitting one child against another. As the wild cards in this process, they can serve to diffuse or aggravate future conflict.

If your parents made a persistent effort to avoid preferential treatment of one child over another, to dispense love and acceptance as equally as possible, to be fair, and to refrain from withholding approval from any of the children, you may have come away with only a small bundle of relatively insignificant resentments. But if you grew up in a family where the children were treated inequitably (whether in reality or perception) or where uncontrollable circumstances dictated an unequal parceling out of valued attributes or attention, then you are probably laden with a heavy burden of sibling rivalry that has the power to cause you real problems today.

•

Sherry's rivalry with her sister, Arlene, has reached epic proportions even though the two women have had almost no contact for many years. Seven years her sister's senior, Sherry was a child of the Depression who was unwanted by her mother but became her father's favorite. She was conceived out of wedlock, an embarrassment to her mother's proper Bostonian family. Her father, whose background was not so lofty, believed his beloved wife would not have married him if she hadn't been pregnant so he felt Sherry to be a gift from the gods.

Sherry and her younger sister grew up feeling little connection with each other. "Arlene was so much younger than I that we never knew each other very well. I left home for college when she was just a young girl. It wasn't until I was an adult that I understood the animosity that she felt for me, and I was completely amazed. It had never occurred to me that she would envy me. After all, Mom doted on her and thought she was perfect. But one day after an argument, Arlene blurted out how men always loved me and rejected her, just like Dad. She said Dad had always used me as the example of what she should be, never gave her compliments, brought her gifts, or helped her with her homework, like he did with me.

"My sister is so angry with me to this day that she has always been a bad seed in my life, causing problems, trying to come between me and our parents, even making a serious attempt to have an affair with my husband and turn my children against me. She has done more to ruin my life than any other person in this world."

Today, many years later, Sherry and Arlene don't speak. In settling their mother's estate, Sherry communicates only through her lawyer. She feels guilty because their mother desperately wanted them to be there for each other and she can't oblige, not after all that has happened. On her deathbed, her mother said, "I want you to remember you have a sister."

"I'd love to forget I even have a sister," Sherry says, "but she's always there in my mind making judgments. I have nightmares about her. Here I am 61 years old and I'm furious at her for doing all those terrible things to me and putting me in this dreadful position. I feel I'm not being a good sister, I'm not being a good daughter, and I'm not being a good person. All because of her."

•

Although many parents try to treat all of their children as evenhandedly and fairly as they possibly can, some definitely play favorites and most are not even aware of it. And even the most insightful and loving of parents can't possibly give every child equal amounts of attention and love with the same intensity at all times. Parental favoritism may be conscious or unconscious, deliberate or unintentional, major or minor, but it inevitably has a tremendous impact on how their children feel about themselves and one another.

All children harbor remarkable sensitivity to their standing in the family and clearly sense everyone's relative rank. From a very early age, they make constant assessments of how they are treated or regarded compared to their brothers and sisters, always acutely aware of who is getting how much of what. And all children, at least at times, think their brothers or sisters are getting more love than they are. Such perceived differences, real or imagined, can produce powerful effects on a child's view of his own worth and his feelings about his siblings forever after.

•

The story of our patient William and his family is one of damaging favoritism and its effect on two sons. John and William, the first two of ten siblings, were born two years apart. John, the firstborn, was the obvious favorite of their father, who planned to pass the family business on to him. The father, a self-made man in the boom years of the Twenties, consolidated his fortune during and after World War II. Extremely shrewd, he ardently believed in the work ethic and his manifest destiny to become rich and powerful. He instilled these beliefs in his children along with a sense of Yankee frugality and an acceptance of hard-drinking socializing.

There was no doubt in his mind that William was born to serve his favored son, John. Together, the two were a formidable pair, schooled in the best Ivy League institutions. As adults, John was to assume the reins of power slowly and William was to engineer the strategies that would expand the business into new and lucrative fields.

They played their parts well although the tension between them was always apparent. Even though everyone close to the brothers advised their father that John was not capable of running the business, Dad refused to recognize it. Meanwhile, William took refuge in his cocktail shaker.

The first big test of John's leadership in the family business occurred during a hostile takeover of a rival company. Although John was foundering, William's maneuvers behind the scenes averted a near disaster. Their father was delighted. The well-oiled machine he had worked so hard to construct performed flawlessly.

In private, Dad gave William credit for his contribution to the deal, and at the same time, cautioned him about his excessive drinking. "I felt minimized and taken for granted, just as I always had," William says. "John was in over his head and I was actually the one who should have been the leader, the chairman of the board, but that wasn't the way Dad wanted it." As John went on to become a powerful person in the boardrooms of corporate America, William's pain increased and so did his drinking.

Suddenly, without warning, their father died. "John was completely devastated, but I felt strangely relieved," said William. "Then I began to feel like a terrible person for feeling that way. I got bloody drunk at the wake." Many powerful people came to pay their respects and John was encouraged to fulfill his father's goal of taking the company public. "People saw how drunk I was and some politely suggested that I mobilize my grief to help John now," William said. "Even now, I was still expected to feel inferior to him. And if I didn't help him become a star, I would not only be a bad brother but a bad son as well."

William continued to find alcohol his only way out as he watched his brother try to control the forces he set in motion to take the company public. Before long, despite tremendous feelings of guilt, he stopped putting any effort into what he saw as John's company, and John became more frazzled without his brother's guidance. He could not understand why their father's death had had such an effect on William and he hoped that William would soon snap back.

But he didn't and it became clear that John would have to carry on alone. Unfortunately, the company became a takeover candidate itself and John was unable to protect it from the inevitable junk bond king who swept in and took over. Meanwhile, William read about the disastrous happenings in the newspapers and kept on drinking.

The alcohol had served its purpose. William could tolerate the world, seeing himself as a weakling and an alcoholic, but not as a vindictive, disloyal, subversive brother.

Now that the father and the business were dead and he no longer had to prop John up from behind the scenes, William was able to shed the disguise. He is a patient in our substance-abuse treatment program and has started to put his life back together, even making plans to start his own business.

Choosing Favorites

It is a rare child who doesn't feel his parents favor a brother or sister over him, or him over them, and the truth is that every parent has a favorite child, the one with whom he or she feels most kindred. Although parents usually protest that they love all of their children the same or each in a different way, they inevitably have unequal feelings about them and, however subtly, treat them differently.

The reasons for parental favoritism may be simple or complex. Sometimes understanding why Mom or Dad loved one child best is confounding until you look beyond the present and examine the influence of ancestral demons. When you do, you will see that favoritism is often based on factors in your parents upbringing and their own sibling relationships.

•

Consider this convoluted case of favoritism. Karen and Ethel were sisters who fought all of their lives until they were 83 and 84, respectively, when something of a miracle occurred. To outsiders, it seemed that they had spent much of their time quarreling with one another and the rest complaining about the other's shortcomings. At family functions, a battle was inevitable and one or the other was sure to storm out with her family in tow.

At age 83, Karen, suffering from depression, came to us, escorted by her younger daughter, Jessica, who had been in therapy with us for some time. Jessica also brought her youngest daughter, Jane. It was a last-ditch attempt to unmuddy very murky waters that were affecting three generations of the family. It was fascinating to see this old woman jumping in to tell her side of a story that took place seven decades ago—as if no time had elapsed.

"My sister Ethel always bossed me around and my mother let her. She got everything first and I was supposed to feel lucky to get her hand-me-downs. When my own two girls were born, I made sure the oldest one didn't get the best of everything like Ethel did. I didn't want my little Jessica to end up the underdog like me. But I see now I've created tremendous hostility between them."

As Karen told us about herself and Ethel, it quickly became clear that Ethel had also identified with her own child who shared her birth order. As the eldest, she bonded with *her* eldest daughter and fought incessantly with her youngest, constantly comparing her to Karen, her nemesis, and assigning to her most of Karen's "hateful" traits.

It also seemed clear when Jessica spoke that this pattern of favoritism was heading into the next generation. "I can see that I'm doing the same thing with my own two children," she said. "I find myself always trying to protect my younger child from the older one. It's like she's me all over again." Obviously, this pattern would be the family's legacy unless they could somehow rid themselves of it, because even the granddaughters were caught up in it.

In our few sessions together, Karen's family talked about feelings they had never before revealed to one another or even admitted to themselves. When they realized how each of them had identified and empathized with the child of her own position, favoring her at the expense of the other, they started to make important changes for the better in the family dynamics.

Gender Generalities

Gender, too, influences parents' feelings about their children. Many mothers feel uncomfortable with sons, anticipating problems because of past experiences in relationships with men. Others favor boys because they don't feel competitive with them and hope they will fulfill their dreams. Many identify with their daughters simply because they are more like themselves. Dads often prefer girls because they feel free to be affectionate with them but don't know how to deal with replicas of themselves. Some, on the other hand, find it easier to get close to their sons because they empathize more easily with a child of their own gender or count on his achievements to provide them with more satisfaction than they derived from their own.

In most families, boys are treated differently than girls. Boys, we have found, are still the most esteemed sex in most families and in some ways tend to be favored over girls. A male child is usually taken more seriously and his success still assumes more importance than that of his sister's. Today, however, it is becoming much more common for girls to openly compete with their brothers, increasing the possibility of intense rivalry because now members of either sex may feel resentment when they are relegated to the inferior position.

•

Favoring one child over another doesn't always reap benefits for the favorite. Paulette found it to be a terrible burden. By the time she was five, she had been dubbed "Sue Barton, R.N.," by her mother, who had had a battle with multiple sclerosis. Her brother, two years younger, was his father's boy.

Paulette was Mom's best friend, companion, maidservant, and confidante. Although her mother didn't have serious repercussions from her illness for many years, she was obsessed with her health and made Paulette feel that if she pulled away from her, she would be responsible for whatever dire results might occur.

"Mother discouraged me from dating and made men, including my dad and brother, look like an awful breed. Girlfriends were tolerated but constantly criticized, making real friendships difficult to maintain," Paulette said recently. "I love my mother but I feel that being her favorite has robbed me of my life."

•

Sometimes a parent finds one child more appealing than another because of their inherent temperaments. It is now almost universally accepted that babies are born with personalities. Some babies are easy, cheerful, and adaptable right from the start, while others are cranky, difficult, slow to warm up, smiling reluctantly and complaining a lot. The first variety is obviously much easier to find charming and lovable. Add to that the fact that, just as with adults, there are some children whom you instinctively like and some who rub you the wrong way.

•

To listen to Meryl, you'd think her first child was a little monster. "Right from the start, Alice was a difficult child. She cried, she screamed, she threw up her milk, she didn't sleep, she didn't smile, and she had a nasty temper." But her second daughter, Diana, born three years later, was an angel who smiled and gurgled and rarely complained. "I felt guilty about it but I couldn't help preferring her, although I've always tried not to show it," Meryl says.

•

Favoritism may be dependent, too, on timing. Were you or your siblings born during good times or bad? Were you a planned baby or the result of an "accident"? Were you conceived in wedlock or out of it? Were you born to young parents or did you arrive late in your parents' reproductive lives? Were there outside circumstances, such as a death in the family, that made you or your sibling more or less accepted than the others? Were your parents contented or miserable with their lives? Although you had no control over the circumstances of your birth, you may still be blessed or damned as the result of events you had no power to change.

The emotional gratification parents seek from their children is another reason for choosing favorites. With their own desires for success and status, they often see their children and their accomplishments as reflections on themselves, so they select the one who seems most likely to help them achieve their goals.

Sometimes, too, a child is favored because of his special talents or abilities. Everybody loves a winner and parents are no exception, especially when their genes produce a genius, a great athlete, an exquisite beauty, a concert pianist. A child's special talent may give rise to exaggerated favoritism as the parents spend much of their time, energy, attention, and money in an effort to help that gifted child reach his or her potential and shower them with reflected glory. Ultimately, they often alienate their other children in the process.

After They've Gone

Many times, the parceling out of favors, both positive and negative, continues long after death as the parental hand reaches out from the grave. Wills are not only financial legacies but emotional ones as well, and while they should not be testaments to parental favoritism, they often are. To adult children, the way the estate is divided up is frequently seen as an expression of what the parents really felt about them, and they tend to view it as the final statement of favoritism. It often is just that.

Variations on a Theme

Favoritism isn't the only variable in a family that can affect the intensity of sibling rivalry. Take, for example, the size of the family. Having only one other child in your household as you are growing up condenses and intensifies the sibling relationship by narrowing the contenders for love and attention. When there is just one brother or sister as your reference point, it makes each of you extremely vulnerable to the emotional impact of the other.

On the other hand, the greater the number of children, the greater the dilution of parental resources. Obviously, parents with a houseful of youngsters have much less time, energy, and money to spend on each child than those with only two or three. Their children soon learn they must battle for these "scarce goods" or learn to do without.

The oldest children frequently assume maternal or paternal roles with the younger ones, taking up the slack for their busy parents, and all of them tend to become dependent upon one another for nurturance, providing yet more opportunities for intense rivalry. The children often divide up into groups, segregating according to age or gender, turning themselves into sets of siblings: the older ones and the younger ones, or the girls and the boys. In a family of two children, it doesn't matter if one is a boy and the other a girl because, as the only ones around, they compete with one another. But in large families over time, the siblings knowingly or unknowingly make choices among the others for rivalries and alliances.

•

Nancy, who has three older sisters and three younger brothers, says that when she was small, she was closest to the brother nearest her age, but as the siblings grew into adolescence, the four girls formed their own airtight alliance that remains to this day. "We are all very close, real friends," she says. "As an adult, I think it's the most wonderful thing in the world to have so many brothers and sisters. I don't think other people understand the security that gives you. Despite all the squabbling when you were kids, and any of the shifting loyalties among you, now you have a built-in support system."

Age Differences

The closer in age you and your siblings are, the more emotional impact you tend to have upon one another and the more intense your involvement is likely to be. Obviously, children close in age are likely to share common experiences and life events because they were both there at the same time, heightening the probability of closeness as well as rivalry. Conversely, the more years that separate you, the less apt you are to be intensely involved.

But that doesn't mean that siblings with many years between them can't feel strong competition with one another, especially when they are the same sex and have other siblings to keep them well connected.

•

Edward, for example, now 30, has always viewed himself as an athlete, a good tennis player and an ace on the basketball court. But his youngest brother Adam, who, at 19, is now taller, better co-ordinated, and more powerful, has already managed to surpass him in both of those sports and is on his way to becoming a star baseball player as well. The rivalry between the two, never before apparent, became overt when Adam started to gain on Edward. Adam is basking in his new glory while Edward is having difficulty dealing with it. "I still see him as the little kid who used to wet his bed. After all, he's eleven years younger than I am. Now he's giving me a hard time on my own turf and I am not enjoying it."

•

The presence of a child who is "different" provides another variable that can intensify sibling rivalry because, by sheer strength and the complicity of the parents, this child often "takes up all the space." He may be so impaired that he is the focus of the entire family, forcing his brothers' or sisters' issues to become relatively unimportant and unattended. If your brother requires a respirator to breathe, your problems with the neighborhood kids will seem too insignificant even to mention because your parents obviously have more important things to worry about. You will feel resentment about the concentration of attention on him and an intense desire to prove that you are just as important, but you probably won't feel free to compete openly and may not even admit to yourself that you feel rivalry with a kid with such major problems.

Rivalry: Good and Bad

The term "sibling rivalry" carries with it negative connotations and to most people it signifies only trouble. Is there nothing positive to say about it?

Yes, there is. In the healthiest sense, sibling rivalry encourages you to try your best and come out a winner. It gives you years of practice in social behavior. And even when the competition is negative, the results can be positive. Above all, it provides you with a sense of belonging. Whatever your brother or sister feels about you, you have his or her attention and that gives you significance and power. It's like the old saying, "It doesn't matter what they say about me, as long as they spell my name right." There is someone out there to whom you are visible, someone who is affected by you, knows your strengths and weaknesses, and regards you as an opponent worthy of battle.

Siblings offer you commonality, a feeling of inclusion and not being alone in the world. They give you a context that makes you feel whole. Not only that, but your siblings' behavior is predictable, familiar, so you know what to expect even when you fight. You go into battle against a brother or a sister using an accepted set of rules and the parameters you learned at home.

The struggle for supremacy you experienced with your siblings is like graduate school for dealing with the competition you will encounter throughout your life. All interaction between brothers and sisters revolves around it and all of the problems that this competition causes later in life can be traced back to unresolved sibling conflicts. Similarly, many of the best moments in life are linked to their successful resolution and the powerful lessons that helped you grow.

If you can't make it vanish, what can you do about sibling rivalry that gets in your way or makes you unhappy? First, you can make it more tolerable by accepting the fact that competition between siblings is absolutely normal and universal and that you are not a bad person because it has flavored the relationship with your brother or sister.

Then, you can work on figuring out the pieces of your family puzzle. Simply becoming aware of what has been going on between you all these years takes some of the pressure off because, as you recognize and incorporate this new information, you are already changing. Why? Because the moment you know something, you start to see things differently. And now, as we will show you, you can then take steps to make changes in the parts of the relationship you don't like.

But first, it is absolutely essential to identify your "sibling of significance," the sibling who will always be your most powerful rival. This is the brother or sister to whom you compare yourself the most, the one who has the most power over your behavior, the one who knows best how to "get your goat," or, just the opposite, the one whose recognition makes you feel especially good about yourself.

3

Your SOS: Identifying Your
Sibling of Significance

No matter how many siblings you have, there is *one* with whom you have felt the most rivalry, with whom you feel the most tension, the most competition, the most threat, and the most connection. There is *one* with whom you most intensely compare yourself, constantly measuring your accomplishments and attributes against his.

This brother or sister can make you feel defenseless, uncomfortable, envious, rejected, angry, inadequate. Or just the opposite—loved, successful, at ease, accepted, worthy. This is the one over whom, usually quite unconsciously, it delights you to triumph and the one whose approval is the most satisfying. Until this special sibling acknowledges your successes, you don't fully appreciate them yourself and something always seems to be missing. A word, a gesture, an offhand remark, a look, and you can feel you've surpassed your greatest expectations—or made a mess of things.

This brother or sister is your SOS, your sibling of significance, the one person who, along with your parents, has had the most effect on who you have turned out to be and the way you behave. Although you may feel this is not true in your case, and you may be the exception to the rule, we encourage you to look deeper because it is a rare person who doesn't have this special relationship with one of the siblings she or he grew up with.

Identifying Your SOS

When there are just two children in your family, your only sibling is automatically your SOS. But when you have a larger family, it may not be so simple to figure out who it is.

Your SOS, your most powerful sibling, is not to be confused with the brother or sister to whom you feel closest or most intimate. Nor is this necessarily the one whom you respect or like the most. Although friendship and rivalry are not mutually exclusive and you may feel very close to your SOS a good part of the time, your feelings toward your other siblings will be much less complicated. With your SOS, the quality of warmth is inevitably flavored by the competition between you, although you may not admit it to yourself. The result is that both of you are always striving to be in control, feeling inadequate when you lose and a sense of satisfaction when you win.

•

To illustrate this concept, we will tell you about Kate, age 68, who came to see us only three months before she had a fatal stroke. She had just discovered her sister had betrayed her and was in a state of deep depression.

From a poor immigrant family, Kate had done well. She was an attractive woman who dressed impeccably and adorned herself with all the status symbols of wealth, from jewelry to couture suits to chauffeured limousines. A woman who was generous and charming, she felt protective of everyone, especially those close to her.

She had, for example, lent her next-door neighbor the money to live on for three months when she lost her job.

"I guess I am a very naïve person, especially about my sisters," Kate said during our first therapy session. "I have never allowed anyone to say anything negative about them and I didn't listen when people, including my husband, warned me about Martina." She had just discovered that Martina, her next-oldest sister with whom she shared a business, had been stealing from the firm for years and had made some illegal deals, placing the business in jeopardy. "If she'd really needed the money, I would have helped her out," she said.

"Martina was the one who started the firm—cosmetics—and I trusted her, even though she was pretty sneaky when we were kids. For instance, I remember the Christmas I caught her stealing things out of our brother's stocking. But it never occurred to me she'd do something like this. In our family, we did well because we took care of each other. Let's face it, we all had our problems. Look at Martina. Her husband is an alcoholic, and her daughter is a mess. The rest of us are grateful to her for bringing us into the business but we've all been afraid to stand up to her. Now I don't know what to do."

Before Kate had time to sort out her feelings about her current situation, she had a massive stroke, and the family gathered at her bedside. There was Martina, of course, her business partner with whom she had worked for many years. Although Martina loved money, she was so afraid of being poor again that she spent as little of it as possible. She had become a miser, and couldn't understand Kate's extravagance. She found nothing wrong with her illegal behavior, which she attributed to "doing business."

Vic, the oldest sibling and the only brother, was at the bedside too. He was the one who helped their mother bring the family to the United States, helped raise his five younger sisters, and actively resented the lower status that came with being a boy in this matriarchal family. Mom, the powerhouse, had little use for men ever since she found her philandering husband with her best friend. After that she saw men as drones to serve her needs. After

Vic's wife had left him and their handicapped son, Martina had taken him into the business too and, in return, he became her ally in many of her nefarious maneuvers.

Lillian was present as well but only in spirit, having died years ago. A financial genius fifteen years Kate's senior, she had adopted Kate as her protégée. She had been a successful self-made woman, smart, courageous, generous, and charming, a woman Kate had always tried to emulate. The leader of the siblings, she would arrive for holiday celebrations laden with gifts for everyone.

Sonya, wedged in between Lillian and Martina and eight years older than Kate, was an tennis player who didn't possess the same quick brain as her sisters. She was taking Kate's illness particularly hard because the two had always been close.

And, of course, there was Martha, the youngest, three years behind Kate, who had become a lawyer but was an immature woman whom none of the others respected. Years ago, the sisters had paid for her legal education. She felt obligated to them but, at the same time, bitterly resentful of her inferior position in the family.

With whom did Kate feel the closest connection? With whom had she compared herself all of her life? Who was her chief competitor, her SOS? Was it Lillian, the sister she respected and emulated the most? No, Lillian was her hero, not her competitor. Was it Sonya, her other favorite sister? No, Sonya was her confidante and friend but not her rival. It wasn't Martha because Kate didn't respect her enough to consider her a real rival. Nor was it Vic, who, as a boy, was not a player in this feminine competition.

It was Martina who was Kate's SOS, the one with whom her rivalry was most intense. "She was always so maternalistic, authoritarian, and superior," Kate said. "When we were kids, she was always telling everyone what to do, ordering us around like she had all the answers. I always hated being told what to do."

Reciprocal Rivalry

Usually, but not always, the choice of SOS is mutual. In most cases, two siblings choose each other as chief competitors and both of them know it. But the relationship need not be reciprocal. This was true for Martina. Instead of choosing Kate or Martha, over whom she had ruled with a special vengeance when they were young, or Vic or Sonya, she focused on Lillian. As the oldest daughter, Lillian was the one on whom the hopes of the family had been pinned. She was the queen in this family and Martina wanted her crown.

When Lillian died prematurely, Martina found herself competing with an invisible opponent, deprived of the chance to even the score with her major competitor. For the rest of her life, she walked in Lillian's very large shadow, forever feeling small and insignificant, no matter what her accomplishments were. No matter how much money she made or saved, it would never be equal to Lillian's fortune. Martina would always know that it was Lillian who directed the sisters into the emerging cosmetics business in the early 1940s and provided the seed capital to get it started. It was Lillian who made the business possible and Martina knew that it would be impossible to control her even if she'd lived, as she did Vic, Sonya, Kate, and Martha.

Carved in Stone

Although alliances and rivalries may fluctuate in the early years of a family's development with the arrivals of new children, alterations in family structure, and the intervention of outside influences, eventually they become permanent. By the time the children in a family are young adults, the territories have become defined and, almost always, each has an identified SOS.

•

Brother Vic had felt the loss of Lillian twice, once from rejection, once from death. Vic had picked her as his main rival right from the start because she took away not only his position as an only child but also his status as the oldest child by being smart and capable— and female. The family had been heavily managed by Vic's emasculating mother, who had led this Catholic family out of Eastern Europe before World War II. At first, the rivalry between Vic and Lillian was reciprocal, but when Sonya was born and emerged as a viable female competitor, Lillian took Sonya on instead. Although Vic never stopped measuring his progress against Lillian, and for all his life saw Lillian as his SOS, Lillian's SOS was Sonya the athlete and *her* goal was to prove herself superior to her.

•

When you are left out of the intense competition among siblings, or have been dumped after having been chosen as an SOS, you can feel profoundly demoralized. No one appreciates the feeling of not being significant enough to be a competitor. Unfortunately for Martha, none of her siblings picked her as their SOS although she secretly competed with Kate, and to this day, feeling unimportant, she spends much of her time trying to pump up her ego.

A Complex Arrangement

"Sibling of significance," or SOS, is a term we have coined to highlight the essential themes of this complex relationship between two people. It combines a sense of danger with the hope of help, the desperation of possible defeat with a feeling of importance, and a desire to come to the rescue when this special person is in trouble. The concept of SOS is an important one to understand because it provides a framework for the exploration of your family dynamics. Although you probably know, if you have two or more siblings, that you don't feel the same way about all of them, you may be most uncomfortable about those unequal feelings. As you examine your relationship with your SOS, you will see that it is absolutely normal and natural to respond differently to each member of your family.

Competitiveness—the fight for superiority over others—is innate to all human beings, especially with siblings of significance and the people who remind you of them. But that doesn't mean the two of you must always be at odds and that you can't be good friends as well as rivals. If you were raised in a functional family, your competitiveness, although it will always be there, is not likely to have become the most important aspect of your relationship with your SOS.

What's more, unless the rivalry has become so intense and out of control that it completely dominates the relationship, having an SOS exerts a positive influence. It provides you with a frame of reference, a way to measure your progress, and one of the few really intimate connections you will ever have. In fact, people who never have a reciprocal SOS—only children or siblings who, like Martha, are the "odd women out" in their families—may well be missing an important developmental ingredient.

More than your other brothers or sisters, your SOS knows your innermost ambitions, longings, deficiencies, and vulnerabilities. He or she knows, for example, that you hid in the closet for seven hours when you were twelve because you were afraid to admit you'd left your bike at school again, that you were arrested at fifteen for dealing drugs, that you'll do anything to avoid confrontation, or that, more than anything else, you fear looking stupid. Your other siblings have a lot of the same information, of course, but they are much less likely to use it and may even have forgotten all about it.

It's very likely that your SOS remembers all of it and knows exactly how to use it. Without realizing it, you may well spend the rest of your days trying to come out ahead of him, in person, in absentia, or even in memory.

•

Kate knew how to push Martina's buttons and she did it constantly. "The one thing that Martina can't stand is when people don't do what she says. It drives her crazy. Even as a child, whenever she told me to do something I was sure to do the opposite. In business, I sometimes do the same kind of thing just to annoy her when she gets too bossy. She can't tolerate it when I don't follow orders." Unfortunately, this rebelliousness carried over to her marriage and drove Kate and her husband apart, when she didn't mean for it to.

In her rivalry for supremacy with Martina, Kate, a popular woman, had also always done her best to make Martina feel inferior to her by painting her as the family bore. A tedious person, Martina was interested only in business, money, and power, and Kate made her the butt of many hilarious tales at family gatherings. The story she liked to tell best was the time Martina was not invited to the senior prom and finally ended up going with her brother, Vic.

•

The stored historical data that each SOS has about the other can be tapped to help each of you understand yourself better and explain some of your fears and inabilities. Or it can serve as an instrument of torture, a weapon used to keep you in a subordinate position, as in the following case.

•

When Mark was growing up as the middle child of three boys, his self-esteem was perilously low for several reasons. His older brother, who was six years older, associated very little with him as a child, then left for prep school at fourteen. "But John, my younger brother, was always on hand to inform me that I was a nerd," Mark says. "John was a year younger than I, but he was just as big, a lot stronger, more coordinated, and very smart. Even though he had chronic asthma—and could always manage to have an attack when necessary—he was into athletics and I was no good at sports. I always was trying my damnedest to do something better than him, but even when I did, he let me know it was accidental and I was still hopeless.

"Today? I try not to talk to him much and I seldom see him because, although I have my own family now and feel competent in my job, all I have to do is see John and there I am—a nerd again. For instance, I mention a problem I have at work and he laughs and says something like, 'My God, Mark, you never could make a decision about anything. When are you going to grow up?' Then he starts telling me about the great things he's doing. It works every time."

•

Margaret, too, is an expert shot. She knows just how to set her older brother off and make him feel inferior. In her rivalry for supremacy with Eric, she has always tried to make him feel like the family outcast. Eric, the oldest of three children, was the dominant sibling during their childhood, but he suffered two breakdowns in adolescence and was hospitalized several times.

Although he has since pulled his life together, Margaret, the next youngest in the family, hasn't let go of her rivalrous feelings. As the only daughter and a middle child, she took on the job of managing everyone's lives. Without realizing it, she has kept Eric from challenging her authority by treating him as an incompetent mental case and reminding him in moments of stress that he doesn't make good decisions. As a result, her brother stays as far away from her as possible, making her feel rejected.

Figuring Out Your SOS

Who is *your* SOS, the one you'd most like to surpass? Finding out is easy if you have only one sibling. That brother or sister will automatically be your SOS. Close as you may be, your one sibling is also your rival and perhaps your model, guide, and eternal frame of reference.

But determining your ultimate rival in a family with more than two children can be tricky, especially if you have learned to conceal your real emotions about family members—from yourself as well as others.

In most cases, two siblings of the same sex choose to be one another's siblings of significance, although they are rarely aware of making that decision. When there is a choice among more than two siblings of the same gender, it's often the one closest in age who is selected for this extra dose of rivalry.

As families grow, the gender of siblings becomes more important in their relationship with one another. In two-child households, gender matters less because the two are forced to compete and compare and so always exert a powerful influence on each other. In a family of three children, however, it assumes more importance. When one of the children is a different sex from the others, that one is almost always the noncontender for major rivalry, regardless of their ages, while the remaining two take each other on.

•

The Green family is a good example. The first two siblings, girls, were bitterly competitive with each other. Spurred on by their mother, a dominant woman who had never achieved her own goals, they took on roles that in the fifties were traditionally male, one becoming a doctor, the other a lawyer.

Robert, their younger brother, never caught up. Although he took on his next-oldest sister as his SOS, she competed with her sister instead. Today, as an adult, he has become the emotional caretaker of his parents. He is deeply resentful of his lack of stature in the family and uses his caretaker role to give him at least a modicum of control over his sisters. He calls his sisters regularly, reporting on their parents' welfare and always trying to control them with guilt by asking whether they have remembered Mom's birthday or what day they plan to visit Dad in the hospital. By making them feel bad for not being "good," he gains a temporary feeling of superiority, when in fact the women see him as little more than a go-fer and a maid.

Speaking the Same Language

The sibling who speaks our language more fluently is more likely to become our SOS than the one who doesn't "get" it. An intellectual sibling, for example, is not apt to choose a jock as an SOS when there is the option of picking another brother or sister who, also an intellectual, readily plugs in to the same system. We all tend to gravitate toward and measure ourselves most intensely against someone who shares our same values.

In the case of Kate's family, almost everyone spoke the same language: money. The acquisition of wealth was the family ethos and the sister who was the most fluent in the "dialect" of money was Lillian. She knew how to make money and her siblings wanted her to show them how she did it and make it happen for them. So the older ones chose her as their SOS, while the others tried to emulate her. The two younger sisters contributed other values—education and social acceptability—but these values were considered valid only if they led to more money.

Kate was caught in between. She coveted wealth but she also placed a high value on education and social status. Her SOS, Martina, however, did not speak that language and so she did not consider Kate's accomplishments to be important, thereby depriving Kate of a feeling of superiority over her.

•

In another family, the common language may be music, for example, or education, or religion, and the siblings who line up under the family banner can relate more easily to one another than to those who don't.

•

The four children in Jonathan's household were raised with the idea that to be literary was to be godly, and three of them marched along this path. The oldest became an agent, the next an editor, while the youngest aspired to be a writer. The second middle child, however, became a stock analyst and he was the one with whom no one lined up. "Even as a child," says Jonathan, "he was different from the rest of us. He was always interested in numbers and facts, while to us, words and feelings were what mattered. We could never really relate to him." And no one chose him as an SOS—he was just too different.

Parental Agendas

In addition to helping determine the values by which all families live, parents set the stage for their children's interactions, encouraging alliances or conflicts to suit their own needs. In the process, they may repress the rivalry between the siblings by not permitting it to be openly expressed ("My children never fight. I have raised them to get along.") or they may escalate it by encouraging their youngsters to compete for their attention.

Sometimes their children are forced into ill-fitting roles or one sibling is subjugated to another, in the name of the greater good of the family. While Lillian was alive, the others were not allowed to cross her. She was the smart one on whom the family relied, especially in the early days in this country. When she became successful, she was treated with great respect and no one could criticize her because their parents had set the parameters of their interactions. That is, until she married a man the family considered unacceptable and feared losing control of her money to the new husband and, later, children.

Then Martina began to compete with her without reproach, and Vic was allowed to badmouth both Lillian and her husband and rise up to dominate the family.

Had Martina tried this before Lillian's marriage, she would have been sternly criticized by her siblings as well as her parents. Kate remembered an occasion from their childhood when everyone was going to a farm to see how cows were milked. In her usual bossy way, Martina tried to decide the order in which the children would be allowed to try milking and she decided it should be from the oldest down. Lillian immediately announced it would be from the littlest up. "Without any discussion, we all went along with Lillian. Her word was law."

Triumph: Surpassing Your SOS

Because nobody likes to feel in the inferior position, those at the bottom of the family ladder strive mightily to climb up and surpass those at the top, especially when they are the siblings of significance. Surpassing your SOS is usually experienced as a great triumph, although it is sometimes flavored with guilt for having downgraded a person whom, under most circumstances, you are supposed to cherish and support. In Kate's family, much as each one wanted to surpass his SOS, it never happened. In the case of Craig and Evan, discussed in the last chapter, Craig did manage to surpass his brother, which made him feel good about himself but at a very high price.

•

Tom is another person who started out in the subordinate position and then managed to snatch the golden ring from his sibling. Tom always felt that Paul, six years his senior and the first of four siblings, was the favored child of the family. "He was the 'king child,' we even called him that, the oldest, the admired and respected big brother, a nice, sweet guy who was everyone's hero. I loved him but he was my competitor. My sister, Dot, who was between the two of us, didn't count because she was a girl. My younger brother, Al, didn't count either. He was born when I was seven and I never paid much attention to him. Besides, if he did something bad, I had the right to slug him for it."

As a child, Tom felt great admiration for Paul. He felt envy too because early on Paul had become a family myth—the one who did everything first and well, the one who had great adventures and close calls with danger. Paul went into the army in World War II, was posted overseas, and came home a hero, at least in his family's eyes. "When I joined the army at the end of the war, I had fantasies of meeting him over there, me the officer, him the sergeant. But of course I was never an officer and I never left the country."

Home again, the brothers became pals, hanging out together, double-dating, and confiding in one another. Still looking up to Paul but unconsciously resentful of his superior status, Tom worked hard to surpass him, never understanding what he was doing until many years later when he was in therapy.

Tom was the first in his family to go to college, to become a professional, to move out of the first-generation culture and the ethnic neighborhood in which they grew up, and to marry "an outsider." But it was many years before he felt he had really surpassed his older brother. "Our kid brother, Al, had a nervous breakdown while he was on vacation in Puerto Rico and we got a call telling us the police were holding him in jail because he'd been found on the beach stark naked.

"My parents were too old and too timid to go. We all turned to Paul. Somebody had to go down there, deal with the doctors and the police, and get him home and into a hospital. Naturally, we expected Paul would be the one because he was always considered to be the leader. But Paul was very reluctant to take the responsibility. He had never been able to tolerate illness, let alone mental illness, and he could not deal with it. So I did it, although I didn't welcome the responsibility either. I got the job done and I knew that I had finally assumed the leadership of the family. Now I was the king and the most respected brother. Paul abdicated and I grabbed the throne. I still feel a little uncomfortable about it. But I watch my back in case Paul ever decides he wants it back. So far he hasn't.

"The interesting thing to me is that, despite all my other achievements, I'd never really felt I'd done anything that great. But now, I'd competed on Paul's turf, and won. For the first time, I felt great."

•

The concept of the "sibling of significance" can help explain why you may feel unfulfilled in spite of your accomplishments. You may strive hard to achieve something and feel exhilarated while you're doing it, but once you've reached your goal, you don't have the sense of satisfaction you expected to have. The reason so many victories may seem hollow is that you have chosen your goal not for yourself, but in the hope that it will allow you to eclipse your rival. Tom did not feel superior to Paul when he became the family's first professional or when he moved out of the old neighborhood—although attaining these goals required monumental amounts of time, energy, and courage—because they had no effect upon his status within the family. Paul was still the most revered and respected sibling. But when Tom assumed Paul's role as family leader, it changed his status immeasurably, catapulting him to the top of the heap.

There are no winners in the rivalry between siblings. It is a mistake, sometimes a tragic mistake, to believe you can be better at being your brothers or sisters than they are at being themselves. The truth is, you can only be better at being *yourself*. In the end, the joy you feel in your own successes comes from "doing your own thing" and accomplishing whatever is important to *you*, rather than what you think will help you win out over your brother or sister. Think about the Olympic champions who have been most successful when they have measured themselves against their own past performances, their own personal bests, and not those of their competitors. If you choose your goals for yourself and not merely to overpower your SOS, your accomplishments will be much more satisfying. And a lot less hollow.

You and Your SOS

By answering the following questions, you can identify your own SOS, if you haven't already spotted this special sibling. You may be very surprised by what you find out.

- As a child, which sibling did you envy the most?

- With which one are you most eager to talk about your triumphs and most hesitant to mention your failures?

- Who is the one you'd secretly like to impress the most?

- Which one can make you feel small and inadequate? Or really great?

- Whose criticism carries the harshest sting?

- Whom do you want most to match or surpass?

- Whom do you think about the most?

- Who was your mom's favorite? Your dad's?

- Who was each sibling's best buddy and worst enemy within the family?

Your answers will point out your SOS. In truth, you have always known who this person is, although you may have never admitted the intensity of the competition between you.

Often disturbing and sometimes amazingly powerful, rivalrous feelings toward your sibling of significance are unavoidable. They are normal and universal, present to one degree or another in every SOS relationship. If you can accept their inevitability, you can begin to shed much of the discomfort, guilt, and negative sense of self you may be harboring about feelings you have labeled "unacceptable" or "disloyal." Admitting that you feel them and realizing that no siblings can completely avoid them are the first steps toward the resolution of your sibling issues.

To figure out the dynamics of the relationship between you and your siblings, you must first figure out who each of you is within the family context, where you fit, what parts you play, what tactics you traditionally use to get what you want, what responses you automatically make to protect your fragile self-esteems against perceived threats. And, you may be amazed when you see how predictable each of you turns out to be.

4

Luck of the Draw: Or,
How Important Is Birth Order?

Many factors have combined to produce *you*, the person you have turned out to be, and your relationship to your brothers or sisters. One of these influences is birth order. Another variable in an intricate set of family dynamics, birth order in itself is not destiny. It does not determine who you or your siblings are, what you think, or how you behave. It doesn't predict your future. Nor does it make you better or worse off then your siblings, although each position has its own special advantages and disadvantages.

But birth order *can* be used to help analyze the general tendencies that are seen most commonly among first, middle, and youngest children, because each group inevitably views the world from its own unique perspective. An awareness of the way people are likely to behave simply because of their placement in the family can help you understand yourself and your siblings better and, in addition, explain some of the roots of your rivalry.

Oldest children, for example, tend to be alike in many ways because they once were the "only game in town," the sole focus of their parents' attention until the arrival of their next sibling. Because, at least at first, they were bigger and stronger than the others and therefore able to dominate, they usually have a more stable image of their identities and capabilities.

Youngest children, on the contrary, have known no time when they had the stage to themselves, facing no competition from larger and more powerful siblings. As a result, they have inferiority complexes lurking beneath their social veneers. They are the babies who yearn for respect, glory, and independence, but at the same time, are filled with self-doubts.

Middle children tend to share some characteristics with youngests because they have spent important developmental years feeling inferior to their older brothers or sisters. But they are different because they were also able to feel superior to those who came along after them. They are the least confident of who they are and often suffer from the poorest self-image.

All oldest and middle children experience "dethronement." They all know what it's like to have the attention and control they've relished taken away from them by a new brother or sister. Now they must make room for an intruder whose arrival, they sense, cannot possibly be in their best interests. Youngest and only children have never had to look over their shoulders fearing someone younger and less capable is overtaking them. They have a position in the family that will never change.

Only children are partially defined by the fact that they have always had their parents' full attention and haven't experienced the problem of surviving in the same household with a rival.

The usual effects of birth order are sometimes diluted by some potentially powerful variables that include the genders of the siblings, their inborn traits, differences in ages and the spacing between them, the size of the family, the "specialness" of any of the siblings, and cases of unusual parental favoritism.

Consider, for example, a family with two children, first a boy and then a girl. If you are the only boy, you are likely to be a mixture of an oldest child *and* an only child. Your sister, since she is the only female, will probably have the characteristics of a young-est *and* an only child.

The same uniqueness may be seen when you are the oldest or the youngest of your gender, because you occupy a position that differentiates you from your siblings. You have a space no other sibling can claim. But if you are the middle girl in an all-girl fam-ily, or the middle boy in a passel of males, you lack the gender distinction that can set you apart.

There are benefits and detriments inherent in all of the family birth positions, although middles frequently start off with more deficits than the others. None of them adds up to happiness or unhappiness, success or failure. And none automatically shapes personality. If it did, life would be much more predictable than it is.

Birth order has been the subject of intense interest ever since Alfred Adler first recognized its significance many decades ago. Using Adler's theories as a lens through which to view sibling re-lationships, we have formulated what we have found to be the most common general characteristics of oldest, youngest, middle, and only children. Only children are included since many sib-lings, because of a gap in age or other special circumstances, acquire some of the perspectives of single children. Twins, however, are not included here as a separate category because twins always know who is the older and the younger of the two of them and usually act accordingly. Besides, twins are worthy of a book of their own.

Viewing your siblings in the context of birth order can give you important insights into why each of you acts the way you do and where some of your conflicts began.

Oldest Children

Oldest siblings expect to be in charge. In fact, they're often quite bossy. They tend to feel capable and superior to their siblings be-cause, at least at the start, they *are*. More powerful than the other children in the family, they see their younger brothers and sisters as less able and worthy of leadership. Throughout their lives, most firstborns seek opportunities to be in charge because they are comfortable with power and know how to use it.

Firstborns often acquire many of the traits typical of only children, depending on the length of time they were around before their siblings came along. They tend to be perfectionistic, conscientious, and intolerant of opposing views, and they feel entitled to a permanent spot on center stage. Their childhoods ended with their dethronement, the birth of their first siblings, when they were promptly turned into role models, surrogate parents, policemen, caretakers, and perhaps even their parents' confidants and advisers.

Although the parents are the ultimate rule makers, oldests are the straw bosses, the right-hand men who are expected to enforce the law, keep order, and set a good example. In return, they must suffer the abuse of the younger children, who may carry on a lifelong battle to undermine their authority.

Because they have spent time alone with their parents and often have been put in charge of younger siblings, they tend to identify with adults and parental authority and to play by the rules. They are company men, who have absorbed the norms and values of society. For them, being with adults is not a treat—it is an accepted way of life, part of a heritage.

•

"When I was a kid, Dad used to take me out to lunch every Saturday while Mom stayed home with my little sister. I felt very special and grown up," relates Francesca. "When we got home, I'd look at my sister disdainfully, feeling enormously superior. She could never sit at a table in a restaurant and conduct herself properly like a big girl. She was only a baby!"

•

Oldests are self-assured and confident, often serious and reserved. They take pride in their accomplishments and are accustomed to enthusiastic support from their parents, so they develop a deep sense of self-worth.

Firstborns are usually conservative, dependable, and highly responsible. They do not care for change, but struggle to keep things just the way they are. Why not, when the trump cards are usually in their hands? They tend to be verbal, academic, and literary, enamored of tradition, customs, and rituals. Their conservatism makes them less creative than younger children, leads them to be compulsive about finishing what they start, and makes them anxious to avoid making mistakes at all costs. They are usually good at carefully gathering and evaluating all aspects of a problem and then making informed decisions.

Oldests believe in "Me first," simply because they were here first and so deserve the privilege of being served first. If life doesn't work out as they expect or they are seriously challenged, however, they often don't know how to adjust. They are not the most adaptable of siblings and often are actually quite fragile, with a tendency to fall apart emotionally when things don't go as planned. They usually find it difficult to take criticism or tolerate their own mistakes, although they can accept the mistakes of others, especially their younger siblings. It's almost as if they expect and relish their sisters' and brothers' inadequacies.

Oldest siblings can easily fall into paternalistic or maternalistic roles and, having become accustomed at least for a while to their parents' constant attention and approval, do well in relationships where they feel superior and dominant. They often don't take kindly to others, such as spouses or bosses, who try to do the same.

Oldests tend not to be emotionally analytical—they usually don't have to be. They know the rules and the appropriate behavior and feel no need to look beneath the surface. While younger siblings may look for and spot ulterior motives in others, oldests rarely wonder "What did she mean by that?" They behave in a straightforward manner and expect others to do the same. They don't like to ask for help but prefer solving their own problems.

Emotionally, oldests have a tendency to repress their feelings and internalize anger.

Firstborn boys are the most prized in many families and are first in line for whatever the family values—property, rank, money, authority, glory. They also have the most expectations to fulfill, which puts them under tremendous pressure. Oldest girls usually get all the responsibilities that go with being the first child but without the doting attention given to boys.

Because oldest siblings feel entitled to take charge and capable of being president, they tend to do well in corporate environments where the hierarchy provides support. On the other hand, they are not as daring and innovative as their younger siblings.

Youngest Children

The youngest siblings in a family have a special position, one that no one else can ever share. They will never be deposed by a new arrival and so they come into a stable world with all the major players firmly in place. They alone among the siblings know exactly with whom they must contend.

But when they enter this stable environment, they are the most incompetent of the siblings, at least for several years, so they also grow up feeling inferior. All human beings start out this way and spend a lifetime striving to prove themselves superior to others. But the feeling is accentuated in youngests who, just because of their birth order, may have an especially strong sense of inferiority that persists throughout their lives. Deep down, a youngest child, whatever his current age, feels everyone is better than he is. That's because youngests get a lot of attention and perhaps adoration but are rarely taken seriously because in comparison to the others who are more mature, they don't do things well. Their older siblings are quick to disparage their accomplishments, and even their parents are not so impressed with what they can do because they've already witnessed these "miracles" with the offspring who arrived before them.

That doesn't mean youngests can't end up feeling able and worthwhile, but beneath the surface there is that niggling doubt about themselves. While an oldest child may develop inferiorities through experience, the youngest acquires his from having been born last. While an oldest or only child usually feels capable by fiat, the youngest must learn to have confidence in her or his own abilities and virtues.

Because they yearn for respect, the goal of youngests is to make a significant contribution to the family and perhaps the world. They desperately want to prove themselves worthy of attention and praise, but are often held back by their self-doubts.

Youngest siblings tend to be remarkably perceptive and observant. This comes from years of watching the mistakes and successes of their older brothers or sisters, finding out which tactics work and which don't, and drawing upon the experiences of their elders to help them shape their own lives. This is an opportunity an oldest child never has.

Youngests often learn to be noncommittal, secretive, indirect, perhaps even devious, because they have painfully discovered that it doesn't pay to let others know too much about them and their ultimate goals. Being open could well be dangerous because the other more powerful people could easily take advantage of them.

"It's not fair!" is the cry of the downtrodden and it is heard most often from youngest siblings who spend many formative years in the iron grip of stronger, larger brothers and sisters.

•

For example, Sheila remembers the fights between her older brother and her mother when Mom found out what he'd been up to at school or with the kids on the block. "She found out because he couldn't keep any secrets," she says, "and then she'd be furious. He was always being punished for something. I learned very early to tell her only what I wanted her to hear." She also realized after much self-examination that she applied this philosophy everywhere, giving other people what they wanted without revealing her own feelings. She was known for her sympathetic ear and eagerness to help other people solve their problems and, in that way, kept the focus off herself. "That's how I stay out of trouble. Nobody has the slightest idea of who I really am. The big problem is that I feel compelled to protect myself and I feel safer that way, but in the end, I never seem to connect with anyone."

•

Growing up as the youngest of the siblings tends to produce people who look to others to take the lead. Little is expected from them and they are so insecure about their own abilities that they are afraid to take total responsibility even though they yearn to feel important and respected. They have an overwhelming desire to be the boss but are afraid they can't handle it. They want to be masters of their own fates and those of the rest of the family as well, aspiring to the power they didn't have as children.

As a result, they sometimes stay at home far too long, unconsciously figuring that, when the older siblings leave the nest, it will be their turn to rule the roost. Instead, they usually spend even more years being babied.

As adults, youngest children are the most striving and competitive of all the siblings because, having felt powerless, their desire to control their environment is tremendous. As the lowest sibling on the totem pole, they feel compelled to rise to the top. Their major goal is to surpass the competition, to be better, to win, no matter the odds.

For this reason, they will test the limits and try to see what they can get away with. They are often the siblings who are the most radical, the most rebellious, the most likely to accept new theories, and the least likely to relate to authority figures. They are the ones who develop new routes, new ways to reach their goals. They can't play by the rules because early on they lacked the equipment with which to compete. If the goal was to see who could run the fastest or write the best or win the contest, they didn't stand a chance. So they interrupted the game by getting sick or hurt—or they changed the rules to suit themselves.

The babies of the family often receive extra doses of affection and attention and, in the eyes of their siblings, are often allowed "to get away with murder" by parents who tend to become more permissive with each child. They are likely to be fun-loving, charming, affectionate, and coy, people who have learned how to get their own way by cajoling and wheedling.

Because youngests are always bucking the system, some of them are easily discouraged and unwilling to challenge others, feeling they can't possibly meet their expectations. Because they expect to lose, they often buckle when faced with the possibility of failure, giving up the fight with less resistance than their tougher siblings.

Youngests usually thrive on attention and are not expert in nurturing others. Although they are trying hard to please, they may not be supersensitive to other people's feelings, simply because, for their own survival, they are focused on striving to do better and better. Instead, they are always concerned about whether they are liked, accepted, respected.

Often the only way youngests can feel important and in control is to be the one who takes care of everyone else, listens to problems, feels bad for those less fortunate, and does "good deeds." Because they have spent so many years in the shadows of older people, they tend to develop excellent listening skills. This, in turn, gives them possession of insider information that can make them quite deadly when they use it in their own service.

Because their problems and needs are frequently trivialized by their older siblings, they often learn to distort the truth, exaggerating their experiences and feelings in an effort to be considered people of consequence.

Creative and imaginative, they are the ones who are likely to become artists, people who are not mainstream, who march to different drummers. Persuasive and charming, they may also make successful salespeople and teachers. Although they are desperate to succeed, they are not comfortable with leadership. Winning the election for president? Great! Overthrowing the incumbents? Wonderful! But being president is not a happy job for most youngest siblings. Although they love having the power, they are often too insecure to enjoy it.

Youngests, in general, are not as trusting as their older brothers or sisters. In fact, they are often frankly suspicious of the intentions of others, having been subjected to the wiles of older siblings who took gleeful advantage of their gullibility and naïveté when they were children. They believe that, given a chance, other people will expose their vulnerabilities, so they are always wary. This tends to make their friendships and love relationships tentative and fraught with mistrust. Patience is the word for developing a relationship with a youngest child.

Because their thoughts are not validated and often denied, the babies of the family are always questioning their own judgment, and this insecurity follows them through life.

Youngest children are more likely to be dependent personalities—far more than oldests, who are accustomed to exploring new territory without a map, and even than middles, who are more experienced in getting along on their own. They discover very early that other people are always willing or even insistent on doing things for them and so there's no need to learn how to do for themselves. The irony here, however, is that youngests may end up controlling their elders by turning them into their servants. There is tremendous power in helplessness.

Middle Children

Middle children come in many varieties. There are middles in a series of same-sex siblings; middles who have both brothers and sisters; middles who are the *only* members of their gender in the group; middles who are the *first* or the *last* members of their own genders; middles in large families; and middles in small families. But they all view life from their special perspective as middles, very different from that of youngests or oldests.

The purest middles are those who are born in the midst of siblings of the same gender. Because these middles are the least differentiated members of a family, they often have the most problems dealing with life right from the start. This undifferentiated and uncomfortable position is infrequent because families aren't typically made up of three or more offspring all of the same sex. Most middle children are *also* the youngest boy or girl, or the oldest boy or girl, or the only boy or girl, providing them with a buffer and a distinction. Middles who achieve differentiation, who are special in some way, usually have an easier time creating a distinctive identity for themselves and figuring out who they are and what they want.

Middles who are the oldest child of their sex but have an older sibling of the opposite sex tend to share the characteristics of middles *and* oldests. And middles who are the youngest child of their sex take on some of the qualities usually seen in youngests.

Nevertheless, middle children (and there may be several of them in a family) tend to have core personalities quite different from the first and the last of the siblings. They usually suffer from lower self-esteem than the others and are frequently the most psychologically vulnerable. They occupy a difficult position, placed at birth in a double bind—plagued by inferiority to those who are older and by superiority to those who come after them. The ground is always shifting beneath their feet and they never have the security of knowing exactly where they fit into the family. While the oldests' primary goal is to rule over everyone and retain their power, and the youngests' aim is to make waves and rise to the top, the middles often feel completely undefined.

If you are a middle child, you will recognize some of these traits in yourself. First of all, middles often feel lost in the shuffle, neglected, left out, consistently upstaged. They feel like outsiders whose problems are not addressed because their parents are too busy focusing on the others. They always have to fight extra hard for their piece of the pie.

A major characteristic is a tendency to be supercautious. Their chief goal in life is to avoid making decisions. They are capable of methodical and fastidious research, examining minute details of a problem as a prelude to decision-making, but then, when the moment of truth arrives, they are unable to reach a conclusion. What they want is for other people to decide for them. That's why they make good brokers, salespeople, or deal makers. They can then present all the options they have so carefully researched and let others make the final call.

Middles who force themselves to make choices, however, are likely to disregard everything they've spent so much time researching and make impulsive decisions that often turn out to be self-sabotaging. Trying to emulate the leadership of the oldest child and the risk-taking of the youngest, those in the middle don't know how to make either quality work for them.

Because they overanalyze and "think too much," middles are procrastinators. They find it almost impossible to come to grips with an action and putting it off is the least uncomfortable way out. Because they blow in the wind, bending this way one moment and that way the next, they are easily influenced and very flexible. They go with the flow. They don't get into arguments because that would mean taking a firm stand.

A handicap, one that accompanies their abhorrence of decisions, is constant second-guessing. Middles are plagued by second thoughts. Should they have done it, should they have waited, should they change their minds, what if, what then? Middles, especially those in same-sex families, often find it difficult to commit themselves to a goal. They may take a job, for example, because it happens to turn up at the right time, or marry someone who pressures them to make the commitment.

Image is very important to them. Because they usually feel ill-defined, they are always seeking to appear solid and "together." Always looking for their own niche in life, they are usually very vulnerable to hurt and rejection. But they try not to show it, covering up with a cool, unemotional exterior.

Middles learn to be negotiators and mediators, even rescuers. They understand compromise and how to give and take. They are congenial, patient, even-tempered, dependable. They tend to be conscientious, careful, and hard-working, but happiest behind the scenes because they desperately fear being seen as "different."

Born diplomats, they do well as social workers, lawyers, arbitrators, and middle managers because they are good listeners and are accustomed to dealing with superiors and subordinates and varying points of view. They are excellent jugglers, a quality perfected in their early years when they were forced to play one sibling off against another to get what they wanted. They have the ability to see all sides of a situation and understand what other people are feeling. They are strong on tact and sensitivity, modest about their own achievements.

Because their position is less clearly defined, middles may look outside the family for their identities. Friendships are very important to them and so they become good team players, getting much of the support they crave from their peers. On the other hand, they are often careful not to let other people get too close to them.

Only Children

If the relationship among siblings is so powerful, so essential to the development of social skills, then how do only children, with no siblings on whom to practice, learn to get along with the competition? Onlies are forced to practice on their parents and sibling substitutes, such as cousins or playmates. Basically, they get their information secondhand, and that can put them at a distinct disadvantage in their relationships with other people. This quality and many other characteristics of onlies may also be seen among oldest siblings with many years separating them from their next brother or sister.

In some ways, only children grow up in the best of all possible worlds. As the oldest and the youngest offspring in their families, they are endowed with the advantages of both without ever having to compete for attention or a distinguishing role. However, they can miss out on learning how to form bonds and alliances, as well as rivalries, with siblings who would have provided them with their "people skills." And they have the disadvantage of going through life burdened by having all of their parents' many expectations laid exclusively on them.

One result of this exclusivity is that only children never learn what it means to share, never experience the pain of not getting what they want because someone else has priority. And, while siblings know that their parents can love more than one child, singles never know what it is like to have an equal rival. Often jealous of people with siblings, they cannot comprehend the strength of the sibling bond.

Single children, however, are superior to most siblings in their ability to establish very powerful friendships that are longlasting and close. One reason is that they understand the vulnerability of their lonely position and yearn for soulmates. Also, they are not on the lookout for the intrigues of sibling relationships and do not, as many brothers and sisters do, see the possibility of betrayal and subversion lurking around every corner. They are usually trusting souls who tend not to be jealous of their friendships or other people's achievements or possessions. They accept others at face value and tend to get along well with other people, especially eldests or only children. In fact, they are often extremely generous and even magnanimous. Most onlies, unaccustomed to constant interaction with siblings, are comfortable with being alone and develop admirable skills for entertaining themselves in their own company.

Similar to oldests in many ways, only children are, in general, conservative. They feel best with order and like things to stay the way they are. They play by the rules and, having spent so much time with adults, develop agreeable ways to relate to adults and tend to identify with parental authority. Frequently, they are extremely successful because they feel entitled to dominate and can easily assume a leadership role. They set high standards for themselves and others and, because they are used to it as the repository of their family's hopes and dreams, are usually well able to deal with pressure. They tend to be reliable, conscientious, self-contained, punctual, even-tempered, and independent, with firm likes and dislikes about which they are extremely articulate and forceful. Their verbal skills are excellent and they are often good debaters.

Like youngest children, they are singlemindedly goal-oriented, but not because they are rebellious or seek to triumph over other people. They simply want what they want and go for it in a direct and straightforward manner, keeping their eyes locked on their objectives. Onlies often give the impression that they are ruthlessly competitive, while in reality they are unconcerned about other contenders. Because they have never had to fight for anything, they expect success. They never look over their shoulders for fear the competition is gaining on them.

Only children—and those who are much older than their siblings—are usually very enthusiastic about whatever interests them, which can be many things, and often become authorities in their field. They have the ability to concentrate intensely while blocking out distractions.

Often narcissistic, self-involved, and unaware of other people's feelings and moods, however, they may feel wounded and confused when they don't get what they want. Having grown up without competition, they don't cope well when they come upon unexpected obstacles blocking their path.

Because onlies had no siblings to take attention away from them (or if attention was purloined, it was not by an equal), everything they did as they were growing up was subject to close scrutiny by adults to whom they looked for approval. As a result of living in a fishbowl, they, like youngests, tend to be protective of their innermost hopes or fears.

Birth Order Helps to Define You

We have been talking here about the most common characteristics of each birth order position. Obviously, things are rarely as simple as they sound, and everyone's sibling situation and position in the family is unique. But birth order is one more tool that can help you understand why you and your siblings, born into the very same families, will never view life in exactly the same ways. Your disparate viewpoints and the parts you play in the family hierarchy, which we will discuss in the next few chapters, have a marked effect on the intensity of the inescapable rivalry between you.

When you understand that oldests, for example, are almost sure to be domineering and self-assured, that youngests usually have a pervasive sense of inferiority and a powerful urge to come out ahead, and that middles tend to have trouble figuring out where they fit in, then you will be better able to tolerate the characteristics that, in your eyes, are your siblings' shortcomings. When you have accepted the fact that your siblings started out in life from a different place, you will see that they can never think or feel just like you. Once you understand this seemingly simplistic but subtle point, you are already in the process of changing your sibling relationships.

5

Why You Are Who You Are: Getting Your Labels

Who are you—your identity and self-esteem—is intimately linked to your relationship with your siblings. It is determined by many interrelated factors that have influenced your development, often in part before you were born.

The key components of your essential identity and personality started with the inherent temperament with which you were born. Added to this are the labels or characteristics identified and assigned to you by the family very early in life. More layers are added by your birth order and gender, and that of each of your siblings, your function in the family, the differences in your ages, plus myriad other factors that differ for every family. These many influences are so interrelated that it's impossible to know which comes first or ends up being the most influential. But all contribute to the development of an identity.

Getting Our Labels

Comparisons between siblings are inevitable, even in the healthiest of families. That's why our lives have barely begun before we are assigned our own labels, a set of attributes that differentiate us from the others, define our relationships, give some order to family life, and make things more predictable. These are the traits that our parents see in us right from the start and that will probably follow us into old age.

Self-identity and the development of personality start taking shape from the moment a child is born, when his family perceives traits in him that tell them—and soon the rest of the world—just who this little person is. The first child in the family serves as a reference point for the next arrivals, as the parents decide, consciously or unconsciously, which child has more or less of each quality than the others. As soon as there is more than one child, the attributes are never again measured in terms of real abilities or qualities alone, but always in comparison to those of the others. Everyone now recognizes who is the *most* anything—industrious, bossy, wise, daring, lazy, attractive—and by the time all the children have been born and labeled, this is that person's territory.

The labels an only child receives are usually top-of-the-line. He gets the qualities his parents value most, at least until dethronement by a sister or brother means he must begin to share them. As each new child comes into the family, the territory is divided up so that each sibling eventually occupies his own separate psychological space. This space or collection of traits, fluid at first, is eventually cemented into permanency when the family is complete.

So, this baby may become "the quiet one," that baby "the pretty one." Another may be promptly considered "the smart one" or "the whiny one." Sometimes, unfortunately, it's "the stupid one" or "the ugly one," usually based on whatever the parents and other family members see that makes them like or dislike a child, from temperament to appearance to resembling someone else in the family. Most of the time, the children soon find themselves possessing many labels all at once, with one child becoming perhaps the quiet, smart, sensitive, empathetic one, while another may be perceived to be the lively, creative, talkative, pretty one.

As long as the traits are fairly appropriate and viewed as valuable and desirable, and as long as there is no strong resentment of one another's designations, it's not too important what labels are pinned on a child. Obviously, nobody labeled "the stupid one" or "the different one" will enjoy that title, and even when the labels seem to be positive, they may rub.

•

Audrey, for example, known as "the smart one," was filled with envy whenever her sister Ruth, "the funny one," got the belly laughs Audrey longed for. "To this day," she says now at 33, "I can't tell a joke. And Ruth, I'm sure, feels her brains are inferior to mine. After all these years, we still want what the other one has."

Different Tags for Different People

No two children receive the very same set of labels and, in most cases, the first arrivals retain those they acquired at the start, while younger siblings are usually seen as having different characteristics. If Jane, for example, has been given the label of conformist, the practical one, the traditional one, the cool one, then her sister Alice is not likely to be known as the conformist or the cool one even if she closely resembles her older sister. She will be something else, perhaps the studious one, or the one with an artistic bent.

Sometimes, however, the labels an eldest sibling has acquired may change, always early in life, when previously assigned attributes are given away to a newcomer.

•

Candy was originally thought of as the pretty one and then lost the coveted position a few years after her sister was born. She remembers when her sister was given the crown as the beauty of the family. "I looked at her and I looked at me when she was about three—I was seven—and I realized she was really pretty and by comparison my looks were only fair. And I began to notice that every time my sister's name was mentioned, my mom tacked the word 'pretty' or 'adorable' onto it, something she never did with mine.

"I secretly began to keep score and I quickly realized that I was right. Mom did think my sister was more beautiful than I was. On the other hand, I was much more sociable and charming. People liked me more than Leigh, who was a real brat. I could live with that."

•

Labels, remarkably self-fulfilling, need not reflect reality, although some of them obviously stem from biological differences in temperament or appearance. A baby born with a placid temperament is not likely to be labeled "the difficult one." On the other hand, a child whose inborn temperament is calm but who suffers from colic during his early months may get a permanent "cranky" or "difficult" label that he doesn't really deserve.

Sometimes these seemingly harmless and innocent labels are based on what the parents *don't* see in their other children. Parents are forever looking for special qualities among their offspring. Most try to encourage the special abilities and aptitudes of each child and are pleased when one excels in one way and another prospers in another, feeling that this makes for less tension and rivalry between them. And, in fact, in healthy families, playing to a child's strengths can be very helpful in a world where there are so many possible routes to achievement.

The catch comes when parents, in their unconscious efforts to divvy up attributes and identify the children, ignore the real potential or true qualities of one child for many reasons. They may be afraid to intrude on another child's turf, often permanently and invalidly coloring each child's view of himself. They may be highly influenced by their own family histories and personal biases.

They may also be acting out of ignorance. All too often the parents are unable to maintain their objectivity and then the labels become divisive. Meting out appropriate labels is a task that few parents carry off without causing jealousy and envy among the children, and responsible parents will try to avoid over-emphasizing even the real attributes of one child because it may diminish the self-esteem of another.

In a perfect world, parents wouldn't attach labels to their children at all, but that is never the case. All parents, even when they make a real effort not to do it, assign identifying traits to their children, qualities that, valid or not, tend to stick to them and color their self-esteem. Awareness of this universal tendency and sensitivity to the problems such labeling may produce, however, can help ward off potentially dangerous blows to their children's fragile egos.

•

Andrew, who was labeled the scholar of his family, longed to be an athlete like his brother Roger. But his athletic abilities were consistently played down in deference to his parents' perception that Roger was the athletic one who was destined to be a star on the ballfield. Perhaps, he realizes now, it was because they wanted Roger, who didn't do as well in school, to have his own field of expertise, an exclusive area that made him feel good about himself.

"I wasn't really that smart," Andrew says, "and the tension that developed in the house when I didn't keep on getting top grades in school was awful. Actually, I had just as much athletic ability as Roger but I was never encouraged to shine in that area."

•

The family's supply of attributes may be doled out in even more subtle ways that emanate from the parents' special internal values or the birth order of their children. Oldest children, as we have discussed, are more likely to be regarded as more responsible and steadfast than youngests are. Youngests tend to be regarded as free spirits. And so they usually turn out that way.

Very often, children receive their identities based on their mother's or father's perception of their own relationships with *their* parents or siblings. A mother may need to see one daughter as a representation of herself, whom she views as quiet, sensible, and dependable. And she may see another daughter as the counterpart of her own sister, who was the irresponsible, fun-loving one.

•

Muriel is a mother who has obviously mixed her feelings about her own child Barbara with those for her sister Janet. She is always astonished by how often she calls her daughter Barbara "Janet." Janet, older by three years, was the wild one, the daredevil, the one who did anything—jumped, skied, tobagganed, rode motorcycles—as long as it was frightening. Muriel, just the opposite, was cautious, unadventurous, and a Mommy's girl. She eventually married a dentist, bought a house down the block from Mom, and had two girls.

Barbara, encouraged by her mother Muriel to be a daredevil, loves physical activity, while Maria, her younger sister, always was a child who much preferred dolls to skates and shopping to exercise. Muriel would tell Maria, "You don't want to get all sweated up. Let's you and Mommy go downtown and buy a new dress for your doll."

When Muriel became our patient, it soon became clear that she had a deep distrust of her sister fostered by her mother who, in turn, had distrusted her own sister. Muriel realized that she was labeling her daughters in just the same rigid manner as her own mother before her. She began to see that her depression and anger were not directed at her sister but rather at her incompetent, needy mother and herself for falling in line.

Forever Yours

Once the labels are divided up among the children in the family, they are likely to stick forever, reinforced by the siblings who take their cues from their parents. If Mom and Dad keep saying Sally is the industrious one and Jeff is mechanically adept, the children will think so too. Each will unconsciously accept those evaluations of himself and the others, then proceed to live accordingly, turning the labels into reality.

Valid or not, what matters is how they are perceived within the family. When parents deemphasize weaknesses and play up strengths among their children, giving each child's traits equal and positive value, they minimize the competition and help keep the rivalry down to a reasonable level. In most households, the siblings are assigned such different territories that they are easily defended against intrusion. But when one child envies the characteristics given to a brother or sister, feeling them to be superior to his own, the relationship almost always becomes rife with rivalry. The same is true when one child is discouraged from competing in an area that's already been reserved for another.

Our labels become who we are even if we don't like them. The differences between us are what distinguish and define us, making each of us feel unique. So we cling to them with remarkable tenacity, fighting off any intrusion into the domains we consider to be our own.

Although Audrey, whom we discussed earlier, has just as good a sense of humor as her older sister Ruth, the family has perpetuated Ruth's reputation as the one with the scintillating personality. Ruth guards her labels closely too, with a tendency, she would be astonished to learn, to interrupt Audrey's stories before she has a chance to finish them. Audrey, meanwhile, always feeling upstaged, takes pride in her identity as the more dignified, intellectual sibling who manages to get a few laughs now and then.

Sometimes our labels don't fit us very well. When you are labeled with traits that don't coincide with reality and don't correspond to your true talents and abilities, you may have trouble seeing yourself as you really are. Believing your labels to be valid, you'll do your best to live up to them, if only because you know this is what is expected of you. Perhaps you are not the genius you have been made out to be. You are going to assume you are really clever but when reality proves otherwise, you will probably be filled with self-doubt and beset with confusion.

Labels take on such enormous power that we define ourselves by them and offer them up as reasons why things haven't gone our way. If you, for example, have been characterized as the lazy one, the procrastinator, the one who tries to avoid responsibility, then you'll undoubtedly become endowed with those qualities. Although you may resent being thought of as lazy, you'll probably live up to the label and blame it for your failures. "Oh, well," you might rationalize, "I've always been pretty laid back. If I really cared and worked harder, I definitely would have made vice-president."

When it looks like a sibling is trying to take over our assigned assets, our designated domains, we put up an enormous battle to hold onto them no matter what, although we undoubtedly don't recognize what we're doing at the time. This can happen in different ways. The rivalry escalates when your sibling can't live up to his own labels and tries to take on someone else's, maybe yours, looking for a better fit. Or it can occur when your brother or sister wants yours as well as his. It is in the unspoken struggle to defend our titles that we perfect the self-protective techniques that we will discuss later. Consider Susan and her sister Eleanor, for example.

•

Susan was always known as the absentminded social butterfly, while Eleanor was the practical one, who could always be counted on to find a solution for every problem. It wasn't until they were adolescents and Eleanor's friends began to outnumber Susan's that their relationship erupted into open warfare. Mom and Dad couldn't understand how two girls from such a nice family could act like such barbarians.

They acted that way because Susan was desperately trying to protect her domain as the popular sister while Eleanor let her know that *she* had all the dates. "I realize now," says Susan, "that every time Eleanor had a friend over or got invited to a party, I went berserk. Suddenly I'd get angry with her for some stupid reason. It didn't matter what it was or if it was even true, like she took my scarf or she messed up my side of the room.

"It was about then that I began collecing guys. I didn't care who they were, I didn't even have to like them, just as long as they called and asked me out. Looking back, I realize it was my way of trying to feel more popular than my sister."

Disparity Spells Trouble

In the healthiest families, each child receives an identity that is valued as much as those of the other siblings, and the best relationships are the ones where there is no obvious favoritism, no constant parental comparisons, and no pitting of one child against another. It's when there is a disparity among the titles, with one child getting labeled with traits that are less esteemed than the other's, that rivalry gets a big boost and relationships between siblings become troublesome, permanently skewing their views of one another and themselves.

•

Maggie grew up as the obedient one, the neat one, the child, her mother bragged, who would come home from an afternoon of play just as clean and neat as when she left. Rhoda, four years older, was the irresponsible daughter, the careless one who returned with scraped knees and muddy clothes. Maggie was not only the obedient one but also the one with the good judgment, the reliable one who never lost her belongings and always did her homework. Rhoda was famous for misplacing her schoolbooks and forgetting the errands she'd been sent to do. Her labels followed her through life and now, at 47, her resentment of Maggie's favored position is still ready to burst through the surface of their usually loving relationship.

"Just last year," says Rhoda, "I was going to a formal wedding and wanted to wear the diamond earrings Mom left to Maggie even though she knew I wanted them. I asked her for them. Maggie said, 'Well, I guess so, but I'd appreciate it if you'd insure them for the night. What if you lose them?' I was really insulted. After all, I'm a grown woman now and very responsible. She's lost plenty of things but nobody ever talks about that."

•

All families place higher values on some attributes than others, and in their hearts, as we said before, all parents have a clear preference among their children. Sometimes one child is the favorite of both mother and father, but more often, each parent favors a different child. The usual result is for the chosen child to assume the attributes and skills of the favoring parent, or the attributes and skills that the parent esteems, in an effort to please or to be as much like that parent as possible. Pleasing this parent becomes more important than anything else because it brings wonderful rewards: love, attention, approval, and possibly material benefits like new toys. The child feels good about behaving in the prescribed way and the system becomes self-generating. Consider one of our patients, who comes from a family where the only thing that really matters is straight "A's."

•

Gary may carry around 325 pounds on a short stubby body and have thin stringy hair, but he has become a successful lawyer and the idol of his mother.

His good-looking brother, meanwhile, has never been able to compete with Gary in brains and has always felt unappreciated and undervalued. He too is successful in his field—jazz guitar—but he was not a dedicated student and was seen from the beginning as a handsome charmer who is not to be taken seriously simply because his special qualities are not the ones that were esteemed at home. As the result of having been shortchanged in parental approval, he acts contemptuous of his fat sloppy brother but feels inferior to him. That's why nothing makes him happier than catching Gary in a mistake and letting him know about it.

What Are Your Labels?

You, like everybody else, have your own individual set of labels, traits distinguishing you from the others, that you were known by within your family. Because they have inevitably played a large part in determining your identity and have surely followed you at least to some degree into adulthood, it's important to identify them. In addition, it helps to identify those that are associated with your brothers and sisters too, because they have profoundly influenced the intensity of your sibling rivalry.

Most people can immediately come up with many of their own labels with little effort. "I was the bad one, the one who gave everybody a hard time. But I was the clever one, too." "I was the quiet one, the good little girl who tried to stay out of trouble." Sometimes, however, the more obscure or less dominant labels are harder to spot or maybe you don't readily admit to them because you don't like them or feel you can't live up to them. To help pinpoint these characteristics that have contributed so powerfully to the making of your personality, answer the following questions as honestly as you can. Use the accompanying list of words for clues, feeling free to add others that apply.

Then decide what your siblings' labels are, and how they compare with yours.

- What traits seem to describe the way your family saw you as a child?

- What traits still describe you in your mind?

- What qualities did you have that your siblings didn't?

- What qualities obviously pleased each of your parents the most?

- What traits displeased them?

- What qualities, positive and negative, would your siblings say you have?

- What qualities given to your siblings would you have liked to have?

- Did you ever think it was unfair that a brother or sister was praised for a quality you thought you had?

- How do you feel your labels compare with those of your siblings?

If you are having difficulty coming up with your labels or those of your siblings, search this list for possibilities. Remember, as you do it, that the tags you received in your early days may not match your real qualities and that you may be quite different from what you have been made out to be. The list may also help you see that, although some of the labels may not have been highly regarded in your own family, they may well be held in great esteem by others.

Intelligent   Unintelligent   Athletic   Unathletic
Creative   Artistic   Attractive   Beautiful   Plain
Obedient   Rebellious   Nonconforming   Ordinary
Quiet   Idealistic   Materialistic   Pragmatic
Opportunistic   Pessimistic   Optimistic   Angry
Cheerful   Charismatic   Depressed   Self-righteous
Greedy   Irritable   Shy   Aggressive   Manipulative
Outgoing   Even-tempered   Self-contained
Self-sufficient   Charming   Competitive   Industrious
Cooperative   Organized   Disorganized   Critical
Responsible   Irresponsible   Understanding   Driven
Punitive   Accepting   Lazy   Good   Bad
Honorable   Underhanded   Gregarious   Moral
Asocial   Devious   Straightforward   Practical   Cool
Talkative   Enthusiastic   Assertive   Feisty   Calm
Generous   Curious   Interfering   Envious
Self-critical   Competent   Incompetent   A leader
A follower   A loner   Well-mannered   Rude
Gentle   Abrasive   Introverted   Thrifty

Labels and Roles

Based on the traits they are perceived to possess, whether or not these labels are valid, all of the children in a family then accumulate certain functions or roles to play within the group, forcing all the players into positions that will almost surely be occupied by them forever. If you are the oldest by several years in your family, for example, and have been labeled sensible, responsible, dependable, you may well be defined by your parents as the sibling who watches over the others. And you will probably never shed this role, no matter how much you may sometimes wish you could be just as carefree and irresponsible as your little brother.

Roles, which we will discuss in the next chapter, are not the same as labels, although the two are easily confused. Think of labels as adjectives, one-dimensional assessments of our qualities that form the delineating infrastructure. Roles are similar to nouns. They are the names given to the functions we take on at home and then tend to perform ever after, whether or not they are appropriate to the situation. Together, our labels and roles define us as players in the family drama, profoundly influencing the relationship between us and our siblings.

Dividing Up the Universe:
Your Role in the Family

"I can't be in the same room with my sister Eileen for five minutes before she's bossing me around," says 29-year-old Margie. "She always thinks she's in charge and the only one who can do anything right. And me, I promptly turn into the little sister who doesn't have a mind of her own. It's infuriating sometimes because, after all, I am a grown woman with a responsible job and supervision over two other people. But sometimes, I have to admit, I like Eileen to make the decisions and take care of things, especially when it comes to Mom and Dad. They have always leaned on her more and that's O.K. with me. Saves me a lot of headaches. Besides, I'm not a person who goes around looking for a lot of responsibility."

•

Take a close look at your family and you will see that you and your siblings are cast in specific roles based in part on the labels that have been pinned on you. Each of you has a unique job assignment, your own territory, that distinguishes you and that you try to keep for yourself.

Roles are nothing more than familiar patterns of behavior that describe the specific functions required for the survival and maintenance of the family. Every family needs these functions, such as caretaking or decision-making, to be provided by its members if it is to operate smoothly so fulfilling the tasks becomes our contribution to the group. The concept of roles supplies a tool for analyzing the function of each of the members of the family, helps us to perceive subtle or elusive family values, and provides clues to the nature of the relationship among the siblings. Of course, every serious book on family psychology discusses roles, but we are applying the construct here in an effort to explain the interactions between siblings.

Every role within the family can have hundreds of potential variations on its main theme. Take, for example the caretaker. The sibling who takes on this role might be the gentle caring Florence Nightingale who wants only to be helpful and kind, or, just the opposite, the domineering tyrant who tells everyone what to do and when to do it. The one who plays the baby might be the perennially helpless whiny kid, or the sweet and charming sibling who tries to entertain, or even the ageless little brat who takes pride in causing chaos.

Roles are inherently neither good nor bad. It is only in the way they are acted out that they may be judged healthy or dysfunctional. If your role is at the healthy end of the spectrum, it will enhance your sense of self and well-being. If it is at the other end, it can create despair and low self-esteem.

Roles can be combined, expanded, or even, under extreme circumstances, exchanged for others. But in most cases, they eventually become so firmly fixed that they are almost immutable. So you—and your siblings—are probably going to remain in your familiar roles for the rest of your lives, both within the family and in every other relationship you may have in the future.

None of us like to think our behavior is predictable or carved in stone, so we tend to brush aside the important insights our roles offer into ourselves and our relationships with other people. But to understand why you and your siblings behave the way you do, it is important to identify them. If you have siblings, you will surely recognize who plays what part and will almost always find some variation of, for example, "the hero," "the caretaker," "the manager," "the forgotten sibling," "the rebel," "the pet," or "the special child."

The Power of the Roles

The power of the roles lies in their ability to keep our focus especially during stressful times, to clarify our actions, to keep order, and to project an identity to which others can respond. Roles impose order on the family, setting up channels of communication, letting everyone know who does what and how each person is expected to behave. In other words, they produce familiarity and predictability. Roles may overlap or may be played by more than one person, but once the last child has been born and the family is complete, they are firmly established and—barring a dramatic intervention—almost always become permanent assignments inside and out of the family context.

Role assignments are made in every family to one degree or another. They are normal and, in healthy families, constructive and useful. They are, in many cases, among the most precious gifts and prizes given by the parent to the child because they provide each of us with a definition.

Although you may wish you had been given a different part, you are probably quite content with the one you've got, if only because you're accustomed to it. This is the role with which you will always feel most comfortable because it is so familiar and, although you may try to abandon it or learn to subdue its effect on your behavior, you'll always tend to fall right back into it, especially when you are under stress, because that's who you really are. It will be expected and accepted, with or without some resentment, by your brothers and sisters who, like everyone else, feel most secure when other people's actions and attitudes are fairly predictable.

If, for example, your role has evolved into caretaker in your family, you undoubtedly take great satisfaction in making sure everyone is getting along nicely. And you would probably put up enormous resistance if your perceived responsibilities were usurped, even though you may tell yourself you'd love to be relieved of them.

If your role in the family has always been as leader or manager, you'll naturally assume you're the one who makes the important decisions. If you have grown up as the family pet, you expect to be fussed over and protected by other people, although you may complain you're not being taken seriously. Most of us, when it comes right down to it, wouldn't exchange our roles, with all their inherent disadvantages and burdens, for others. Nor *can* we without tremendous effort and upheaval. But we *can* turn these negative roles into positive ones; we can learn to make them more effective and satisfying, as in this case:

•

Julia, a very competent 41-year-old executive secretary for the chief operating officer of a major conglomerate, fills the caretaker slot in her family. "I've always been the one who remembers everybody's birthdays and anniversaries and makes the parties. I remember when I was eight I found an old date book of my mom's and thought I'd found a treasure. It helped me keep track of important events like birthdays and remind everyone beforehand. It was a source of power that made me feel important.

"Now I'm the one who takes care of people when they're in trouble and invites everybody to my house for all the holidays because otherwise they'd never get around to it. They rely on me."

This year, Julia was feeling resentful because, with three children and an unemployed husband, she felt she was still expected to have the whole family for Thanksgiving dinner and, no doubt,

Christmas as well. She was feeling overworked, unappreciated, and stressed out, both at home and at work.

When her new sister-in-law offered to cook dinner on Thanksgiving to take the burden off her, Julia said "Great!" but soon she found herself feeling depressed. "I had trouble sleeping that night. It's crazy. Finally somebody wants to take over some of the load, and how do I feel? Like she's butting into my business and trying to take over my job!" Julia didn't consciously want to shoulder all the work and responsibility in the family and, in fact, found it too much for her. But she didn't know how else to behave. It was important for Julia to host the traditional family meal, and to receive credit for it. After all, in her mind, "It's not Thanksgiving unless it's at my house." But she realized she could serve potluck style and ask everyone to bring a dish. That way she's still in charge, but she's not shouldering the complete burden herself. She can also ask her husband to help. It takes courage to turn a negative role into a positive one, but Julia is realizing that she can make her role work for her.

Dividing Up the Territory

Springing from the unique needs of each family, roles are first doled out by the parents and then reinforced through interaction among the siblings until they become completely entrenched. If your parents have given you a function that matches your labels as well as your innate abilities, then you will probably find it comfortable and not overly restricting. It gives you inner strength and it helps to define you to yourself and the rest of the world.

•

"In our family," reports Joyce, "my brother was obviously the caretaker, for me as well as our parents. Only sixteen months older than me, Bobby was blond and gorgeous while I was sickly and dark and never liked the way I looked. He was the preferred child, not only because he was the boy and beautiful, but also because he was so responsible and eager to please. He was very orderly and he helped around the house much more than I did. What's more, he took everybody's problems to heart and tried to solve them. He was very much my protector and always there, literally, to fight my battles. I remember in school, when I got in trouble, they always sent down for Bobby instead of calling my mother.

"I loved him even though I felt so inadequate and inferior to him. And that's the way it's been all of our lives. Although in many ways I have been much more successful than he has, he's always been right there ready to serve, especially since his marriage broke up and he's alone again. His wife used to complain that he spent more time worrying about us than her. I'm the one with the secure marriage, the money, and the children, but he's the one who still worries about me and everybody else. If you ask Bobby for help, you'll get it. I'm helpful too but my motive isn't always that altruistic—I recognize that my main reason for going out of my way is to make people like me."

•

In Connie's case, she did not take on the caretaker role in her household even though she was the oldest of three children.

Instead, Connie was the family hero, her father's favorite, who was treated almost as an only child. "To my father, I was the only one who existed and my mother didn't pay much attention to any of us. My brother, two years younger, and my sister, two years younger than him, were superfluous in that house, although I didn't understand that until we were grown up. I was smart, pretty, and always doing something to attract attention. Everyone thought I was fearless and could do anything.

"Looking back, of course those two kids hated me, but it didn't occur to me then. My brother was a typical middle child—he lost out. He was the black sheep. He wasn't good in school, had a hard time with reading. He could fix anything, but my father didn't value that. He was always a skinny, fearful kid, kind of shivery, and I was held up to him as an example of what he should have been. My sister was compared to me too and she never measured up either. She was the baby and we all treated her like an incompetent.

"Now here I am over sixty and trying to make sense out of all this. It's not easy. When I least expect it, I can see my sister's rage coming through. For example, when I go back home to visit, she's sure to get sick the day I arrive so she can't pick me up at the airport. My brother? He left home as fast as he could, got married, and joined his wife's family. I don't hear from him much. He's my brother and I don't hate him and I don't love him, and yet I still have memories of this little kid with big sad eyes and I'm sorry."

•

A family is much more than merely a collection of individuals. It is an entity of its own and everyone in it works together to move it forward and help it accomplish its goals, whatever they are.

The most elementary goals of every family are survival, procreation, and improvement of the lot of each succeeding generation. In addition, every family develops its own special agenda although that agenda is not always readily apparent. The accumulation of money may be one family's primary goal; in another, it could be the desire to be liked and respected. The most important goal may be to turn every child into a professional, or to make sure everyone gets into the best schools and collects academic degrees. The Kennedys of Massachusetts are a good example of a family with clear goals. They were inspired to seek political power.

A family's goals may simply be to survive emotionally and financially and to make sure the children do better than the parents. In most cases, the parents' major goal is to raise children who will be successful and independent and make them proud— and will be around to provide them with support and assistance in their old age.

Who Gets What and Why?

You are cast in your role in the family through an intricate psychological process, directed by forces that are almost always unconscious and often fraught with powerfully conflicted emotions. The roles are delegated according to the parents' needs, the children's actual abilities and labels, and the mother's and father's views of these traits. At the same time, they are intended to promote the family values that, projected onto the children, form an agenda for the next generation.

The children are expected to accept their roles, internalize them, and accommodate to them, after trying them on for size and fit and looking for parts they can play. In most cases, they take to the roles that feel right to them, the ones that suit their natural abilities and give them some status and clout within the group.

Siblings as well as parents have an important influence on what roles each of them takes, unwittingly encouraging, demanding, cajoling one another into them. Just by looking up to a big sister who takes care of them and admiring her abilities to cope with crises, for example, younger siblings can make her feel it is suitable for her to take on responsibility while the others have fun.

At the same time, all of the family members guard their own turf, which, they feel, is their exclusive territory.

•

"I remember one time when I was about six and I decided to be like my big sister, June," was the story one patient told. "I found Mom crying in the kitchen again. I didn't know what was going on but I put my arm around her and said, 'Don't cry, Mommy. Everything's O.K.,' just the way June always did. June, who was about twelve then, walked in right behind me and said that the two of us were really embarrassing and nauseating. That remark along with a scornful look made it perfectly clear that it was her job to take care of Mom, not mine, and I was intruding on her territory."

•

Often, as in this case, birth order has made some roles obvious: Older children are much more likely to be given leadership or care-taking parts than the others, while middles are often the mediators, and the youngests tend to become the rebels or family pets. In addition, the order in which the children were born makes some functions less available to the younger siblings because these roles may have already been handed out. A younger sibling doesn't stand a chance of getting them unless he is especially clever or his parents have reserved a certain role for that particular child.

•

Andy wished he could be assertive and forceful but it was obvious from the start that his brother Peter was the leader in his family. Trying to explain the difference between them, he said, "I remember walking into the kitchen to feed the dog and thinking I could never stand up to my parents the way Peter did. He was only nine, two years older than me, and yet he was much more mature. He was a leader, something I could never be. My parents patted me on the head but they respected him. So I ended up making myself indispensable by anticipating their wishes. Peter was too busy with his own interests to do that."

•

Even the number of siblings alters the options for the parceling out of roles. Generally speaking, the more siblings, the more specific the functions each takes on. Sometimes, just as with labels, two or three children may get the same basic role, with each performing different aspects of it. In small families, however, some of the roles have no takers at all or siblings have to assume more than one.

•

In the Batali family, for example, there were ten children, all separated by two years. The eldest, Diane, was Mommy's surrogate for the next four youngsters, but Irene, the fifth down, was Mommy's surrogate for the youngest four. Both were considered caretakers but Diane was head caretaker and Irene always had to check in with her. When their parents became old and infirm, Diane was the one who ascribed the caretaker role to Irene for Dad, while she looked after Mom.

•

Gender, too, determines the possibilities, with boys more likely to be family heroes and girls more often placed in the position of caretaker.

•

Miriam was older by five years than her brother Josh, but in this orthodox Jewish family, there was no way she could be the star. Josh, although he was much less talented, was the one Dad took into his business, the one everyone respected most, simply because he was the male. No one, even for a second, considered Miriam to be eligible for the same respect and admiration.

In the family, all the good suggestions were attributed to Josh. Although Miriam was the one who suggested moving to the suburbs, Josh got the credit. As Mom said, "We were lucky to have a son with such a clear head on his shoulders. He made us move just before the neighborhood went bad." Miriam didn't even get the credit for starting her own baking business. Instead, the success of the company was attributed to her husband and even she saw the logic of that. Miriam too had accepted that all good ideas emanated from men, so she never allowed herself to feel intelligent. She denied she had anything to do with the company's success, just feeling lucky to have such a smart brother and husband.

•

Over the years, all of the siblings become better at playing their parts. In their inborn desire to be masterful, they develop them, edit them, and incorporate little nuances when they prove successful, until eventually the performances become perfected and second nature.

The role you have been given or that you have assumed in your family is not a haphazard choice, but the result of myriad expectations and needs. If you were chosen to be the hero or the manager or the pet, there was a need for someone like that in your family, just as there may have been for a scapegoat.

•

Alexander was a scapegoat, seen from the start as a difficult child who caused nothing but trouble. Cast as the rebel, the bad kid, he was blamed for the family's problems—an alcoholic father, an enabling mother, constant arguments, and a disintegrating marriage— and he did his job well. He perfected his tantrums, got into fights, disrupted the classroom, and learned to perform outrageous acts on cue—like swallowing the fish, drawing on the walls, breaking a dish—when he sensed tension and imminent chaos in the house.

Unconsciously cast in this role by his parents, he made himself the focus of the family, doing drugs at fifteen and becoming dependent on alcohol before he was twenty-five. Meanwhile, the family continued to believe they would have been perfectly happy if it hadn't been for their problem child. It wasn't until many years later that Alex began to understand that he had simply been following orders. He had accepted his role and he played it very well. You may wonder why he would assume such an unpleasant role. He was rewarded with a feeling of being the glue of the family, the protector of the peace, and the object of an inordinate amount of attention.

•

In Benjamin's case, the major goal of his dominant mother, frustrated in her own attempts to make it in the traditionally male-oriented world in which she grew up, was to make sure that her daughters did the job for her. Her two girls were assigned the role of family heroes, superkids who responded by becoming, respectively, a doctor and a lawyer.

The unspoken demand on Benjamin, the lastborn, a quiet little boy, was to facilitate his sisters' rise to the top—and that's what he did. Now a midlevel executive in a large corporation, married, the father of three children, he became the caretaker/manager who took over the job of dealing with his mother's rollercoaster emotions so his sisters would be free to carry out their roles as heroes.

The only way you can see the importance of a person's role is by removing them from the mix. What if Benjamin hadn't played his part? His sisters wouldn't have had as much time to focus on their careers, and the dynamics of the entire family would have been different.

Rating the Roles

Every role in a family gets a status rating based on the family goals and the values held especially dear by the parents, who look to their children to carry them on. If, for example, a parent's primary goal is to propagate the family name, then the caretaking role becomes the most desirable one. If it values interdependency and togetherness above all else, then the role of the pet rises in esteem because the pet's job is to shift the focus from problems and make everyone feel united in their love for him.

•

In the Carter family's case, the primary values were professionalism and education. An intellectual blue-collar worker who never completed college himself, Dan Carter was determined that his three children would become respected and well-paid, people with solid professions who would always be in demand.

When Dan's wife, Anne, became ill, 14-year-old Dolores was the one who took over the household chores, cooking the meals, tending to her mother, watching over her younger brothers. Bert, the youngest, who was very handsome, sweet, sensitive, and the repository of everyone's confidences, was alternately coddled and forgotten, while Donny understood that he was born to shine, to be a star and a leader and to follow the rules at home.

It all worked out as planned. Donny became a lawyer to whom everyone comes for advice, Dolores a nurse who puts her caretaking abilities to good use, and Bert a psychiatrist, all of them feeling comfortable with their roles because, in large part, without consciously thinking about it, their parents made a good match between their innate skills and their expected behaviors.

•

Specific roles may be ascribed to certain children in the family in an effort to re-create—or to avoid—the patterns of the parents' own childhoods. In the Cushing family, although she would deny it, the two children were assigned by their mother Grace to the same roles she and her brother Steve had played. The first child, a boy, was looked upon as the leader-hero burdened with high expectations of achievement, while the second, a girl, was relegated to the role of The Baby who required her mother's protection and constant solicitude. When Grace realized how, without thinking, she had identified her daughter with herself and her son with her adored but rivalrous brother, she said, "There's nothing wrong with that. I was perfectly happy as a child and I'm sure my children will survive very well."

•

The unconscious assignment of the parts we play within the family and, by extension, in life, frequently stem too from parental favoritism, with the best roles reserved for the most favored child, the worst for the least.

•

For example, Sean and Teresa, both older siblings themselves, have always identified with their oldest child Sean, Junior, favoring him over his brother, Anthony. Delighted with him, they were continually disappointed in Anthony, who has rewarded them in his adolescence by turning to drugs. Although they have sought therapy to help them deal with him, for a long time they were unable to acknowledge the favoritism that was so obvious to us. Sean, Senior, said, "It was hard for Anthony because Sean was the perfect child who could do everything right. He was a great athlete, an 'A' student, and so handsome that Anthony hardly stood a chance."

To us, Anthony was also smart, talented, and capable, as well as good-looking. He stood a chance—but not with his parents, who didn't realize they were dedicated to making sure he did not surpass his brother.

Burdensome Roles

A role is dysfunctional when it interferes with our ability to enjoy life, when it produces a feeling of inadequacy rather than high self-esteem, when it makes us feel we are not allowed to develop our potential, when we feel discontented or overly burdened, when we are seriously jealous or envious of our sibling(s), or when we think they got all the benefits and accolades in the family.

Our roles in the family may also become dysfunctional and overwhelming when they become much too important at an early age. Alexander, the boy who almost from birth became the scapegoat to take attention away from his parents' problems, would have gotten along very well playing the part of a "normal" rebel. But he was cast as the black sheep, an intensification of the rebel role, and this has caused him nothing but grief. Now he must change his views of himself and modify his self-destructive style if he is ever to live a satisfying life.

•

Marianne had a similar problem. When she was only 13, her mother became seriously ill and she assumed the responsibility of running the household in her place. This meant that the role she already had among the siblings, the caretaker, became disproportionately burdensome, so much so that it completely consumed

her adolescent life. Forced to take over the housework, the cooking, the responsibility for two younger sisters, Marianne had little
time left for normal teenage activities.

Her 15-year-old brother Eric, however, who was cast as the
family hero, found that his job description remained exactly the
same as it had always been. In fact, it was enhanced now because
everyone was delighted to be distracted by his achievements.

But suppose the problem had been different. Suppose the children's mother had not become desperately ill but instead their
father had lost his job and couldn't pay the rent. Then Eric,
forced to leave school and get a job to help support the family,
might have found that his role as hero was then blown out of all
proportion, changing the course of his life, while Marianne's part
would have probably stayed as it had always been.

Does It Work in the Outside World?

Sometimes the role a sibling has been given serves its function
beautifully within the family structure but is a disaster in the outside world. While healthy roles prepare us for life beyond the confines of the family, giving us a comfortable part to play wherever
we go, a role carried to extremes can make life very difficult when
we leave home.

A person who becomes the family "manager/caretaker," for example, in a household that required someone to assume this role
so that the family could function adequately, can be so overbearing with friends and fellow workers that he will soon be unacceptable to them if he doesn't modify his behavior. The troublemaker
who evolved because the family needed distraction from serious
parental problems may find that the role did its job very nicely
there. But if he remains forever locked into being a far-out rebel,
he may end up dropping out of school, becoming a drug addict, or
robbing banks for a living. The role of the family "screw-up" is
obviously dysfunctional when it leaves its owner unable to function competitively anywhere else.

Often, however, the pattern of behavior we develop at home, extreme or not, does its job on the outside as well as at home.

•

Babs, for example, was locked into her stifling role as the one who managed everything in her parents' two-career household. She was the organized, cautious, self-sacrificing sister who saw to it that her younger sister, Judy, a helpless piece of fluff, and her brother, John, a workaholic who had to be dragged from his homework to the dinner table, got to school on time, did their chores, and wore clean clothes.

Now that she is married to Don, a highly successful physician with little time for coping with his own personal and social needs, Babs's organizational talents are greatly and openly appreciated. "Babs takes care of everything," he tells everyone while Babs beams. "I couldn't get along without her." Babs has made her traditional role pay off.

•

If, as an adult, you make an attempt to reject your assigned role, redefine it, or take on someone else's, you can expect negative feedback from your siblings and anyone else who has developed an investment in your usual behavior pattern. The others may simply be resisting change or they may subconsciously understand that they have reaped benefits from the functions you have always played within the family.

Besides, they may realize, perhaps unconsciously, that *somebody* may have to do your job if you abandon it, filling the gap you are threatening to leave unoccupied. Some roles are absolutely necessary for a family's survival. If you decide not to be the caretaker any longer, for example, one of your other siblings must take on that job and will probably not be very happy about it. Your brothers or sisters much prefer to retain the status quo, attempting to keep you plugged into the behavior they know so well and may desperately need. If you change your stripes, they will be forced to change theirs.

•

Consider Maria's situation. Maria always willingly played the caretaker in her family, freeing her sister, the family rebel/pet, from the day-to-day burden of their aging father and dependent mother. But when she developed a chronic illness and couldn't cope with being the exclusive arbitrator and workhorse for all of the familial problems, she turned to her sister, Tess. "I'm feeling overwhelmed and I haven't got the energy to deal with all of this. You've got to help me," she told her. "Of course I will," Tess replied, like a loyal and supportive sister.

But she couldn't manage it and she quickly reverted to her old dependent role of the child who expected service and little responsibility, all the while proclaiming how much she was doing for everyone. Nor could their parents change their habits. Although they tried not to lean on Maria as much, they continued to count on her and to excuse their pampered younger child as they always had. And Maria, who had asked for help but in her heart really didn't want it because she gained much of her self-esteem from her role as the one who took care of things, complained about her burdens but continued to do the worrying and the coping because it felt natural and normal. Meanwhile, in a move that occurs frequently when one member of the family can't fulfill her traditional role, she compensated for her lack of strength by recruiting her husband, a willing participant, to temporarily take over her job as family caretaker.

•

Peg, the youngest of four siblings, grew up in a rigid moralistic Catholic family where the children were expected to leave home only after marriage and, until then, to adhere aggressively to the tenets of the church. Peg's assignment was to be the good daughter who took care of her parents after the others had left to start their own families, and she played it to the hilt for many years, even preparing for a while to become a nun. But she managed to alienate the entire family when, feeling resentful of the responsibility, she began drinking heavily. Finally, with the help of therapy, she stopped drinking, moved out of her parents' house, and, to top it off, became involved with a divorced man, a recovering alcoholic she'd met at an AA meeting.

Unaware of their real motivation, the entire family felt compelled to convince Peg, for her own good, to return to her former state of grace as the perfect sister. Why? Because they needed her to fulfill the functions she had always played in that role. Her sister, the sibling closest to her in age and always her fiercest competitor, took it upon herself to straighten her out. Whenever she fell down on the job—as she did with great flourish during her drinking days and now even more, from the sister's point of view, when she tried to separate herself from the family's expectations—Martha had always been the first to point out her shortcomings.

One night Martha spent more than two hours exhorting Peg to clean up her act, saying, "I pray to God that you change back to the sister I know. People always said what a great sister I had. I want you to be the old Peg again, the one everybody loved. You are breaking Mom's heart, you know, and if she has a heart attack it will be your fault. When you moved out, she cried for days. This has always been a really close family and you are destroying us."

Peg, overburdened by the responsibility thrust upon her, is gradually growing healthy enough to realize that she must be free of the family's shackles. Even so, she worries that perhaps she is becoming a mean and selfish person and that her sister is right. Peg had to learn how to use her "goodness" not only in the service of the family, but as a tool for her own purposes, which include living her own life. She does not have to accept her sister's interpretation of her behavior; on the contrary, she can point out that Mom is perfectly healthy and Dad needs to get out and do things for himself.

•

If your family has given you an appropriate role, one that realistically suits your abilities, talents, and attributes, you're likely to wear it comfortably and make it work for you. In fact, it will help you develop your sense of self-identity.

What's Your Role?

Now try to make an honest assessment of your family. What was the family striving for and how did each of you fit into the scheme of things? What is your special family function? What parts do your siblings typically play?

Try a few of the following roles on for size. Keep in mind that all of the examples given here are presented as stereotypes—the most common patterns and extremes of attitude and behavior—and therefore are not expected to fit you perfectly. However, you will see yourself and your siblings somewhere within these general parameters. Perhaps your behavior encompasses characteristics frequently seen in a couple of roles, or maybe similar roles will be played by more than one of your siblings. But most likely you will find fairly accurate descriptions of your lifelong places within the family. Which one you play isn't as important as what you eventually make out of it. Every one of them can be seen, by you and those who interact with you, as a benefit or a detriment to a satisfying life.

The Caretaker

Caretakers feel responsible for everything and everyone. They are the ones to whom the others go in time of trouble, the siblings who pick up the pieces for everyone else, putting other people's needs before their own. Usually leaders among the siblings, caretakers tend to live by a firm set of morals. They try very hard to do what is "right" and end up making a lot of the family's decisions.

Because caretakers feel that other people can't always be counted on to take care of themselves or to do the right thing at the right time, they stand ready to do it for them and to discourage anyone who tries to take over some of the responsibility. "No, no," they say, "leave it to me. I'll do it." At the same time, they are usually quick to complain that they are stuck with all the work and often point the finger at those who are not doing their share.

In general, caretakers are good people, generous, helpful, reliable, and responsible, the ones who will always pitch in when needed. They are the siblings who will drop everything to drive you to your doctor's appointment, who will be there with plenty of advice when you have a problem, and who will visit you, perhaps with a pot of chicken soup, when you're sick. For sure, they are the ones who will take care of Mother in her dotage. Being good to others makes caretakers feel important and in control of their own lives, and, at the same time, gives them a sense of identity and mission.

Caretakers, on the other hand, seek constant approval and tend to feel inadequate, fearful, and guilty. They can never do enough or achieve enough, in their own minds, to prove their worth to their families and so they keep trying harder. They tend to become workaholics and control freaks who find it difficult to accept their own mistakes and who view themselves as responsible for everything. They often spend so much time attending to other people's needs that they can't manage to accomplish their own agendas. And, of course, they never like to ask for help nor can they accept it. To them, that is an admission of personal failure.

People who assume the role of caretaker often have many admirers but few close friends because they are usually competitive, perfectionistic, controlling, and expert at getting approval from higher authority. They tend to marry dependent personalities who require support and constant stroking but who, in the end, often tire of their partner's controlling hand even as they rely upon it.

The ultimate challenge for people who play caretaker is to share power and at the same time acknowledge their own vulnerabilities. As parents, they are hard-pressed to allow their children to make independent decisions, instead smothering them with concern and assistance and making them feel ungrateful if they strive for independence. In fact, taken to their extreme, caretakers can easily turn into martyrs.

Also, at the far end of the spectrum, the caretaking role can be onerous, limiting, and demanding.

The Manager

Managers, unlike caretakers, do not accept hands-on responsibility for the welfare of the others. They are the "Lords of the Manor," who make the rules about what should be done and then assign other people to carry them out. Managers, for example, wouldn't take their ailing aging mothers into their home and care for them day after day. Instead, they would decide it's best for Mother to move in with *you*, although they, of course, would be perfectly willing to be executor of the will.

Managers, almost always the eldest of the siblings or the eldest of the most esteemed sex in the family, have no hesitation about taking on responsibility. Like King Solomon, they are the pragmatic decision-makers who carefully deliberate on every issue and are proud of their ability to come to hard, equitable, reasonable positions. The most admired of the pack, they steer the family along the right paths and expect the rest of the group to follow without question. They think everything out thoroughly and are never given to flighty or impulsive moves. They are, in general, very fair and exceedingly pragmatic.

Managers are ready to manage the lives not only of their siblings but their co-workers, employees, spouses, friends, relatives, and acquaintances who can't be counted on to make their own decisions in an efficient manner.

•

Lawrence is a prototype manager. Learning of an elderly neighbor's problems with Social Security, Lawrence took over. When his local automobile service-station owner wanted to take on new partners, he drew up the contract. When his sister's husband died, he took charge of her finances, outlining exactly what she had to live on and how she should use it. He devotes considerable time to these endeavors and makes sure all the details are beyond question, but he is also quick to become impatient with his troops when they don't heed his advice correctly or move along at the proper speed. Nor does he put up with opposition to his views.

•

Unlike caretakers, whose time is not considered very valuable and who are expected to put other people's needs before their own, managers are busy people who deem their time precious and thus do not spare much of it per problem. However, they know everyone's business, and the little time they do apply to family matters is almost always greatly appreciated by the others.

A major trait shared by managers at the extreme end of the spectrum is an inability to develop emotional closeness with other people. Often greatly admired but hard to love, they may feel needed and important but rarely develop a sense of intimacy. For that reason, when things go badly, there's no one they feel free to turn to for support. Besides, because they must always feel in control, they can't accept help even when it is offered.

Control is what they want most, followed by self-importance and demand for respect. In the extreme, they tend to be brittle people who are easily offended and readily annoyed. Their attitude exudes superiority, tending to make those around them feel like inadequate children. Because of their apparent strength and air of certainty, they tend to attract the helpless and the feeble as well as the users, and, in the long run, frequently end up feeling overburdened and taken for granted. What's more, they complain, nobody's worrying about *them*.

•

In therapy, Scott admitted that he feels put upon. "I'm responsible for everything and everyone. No one moves in my family without consulting me. I feel like I've never been allowed to be a child, carefree and happy, because I'm supposed to be sensible and alert. I'm not allowed to make mistakes either. My kid sister to this day tells people that my decision that she should go to an in-town college rather than go away to school has ruined her whole life. What if I make a wrong choice for my parents' retirement plans or my brother's estate planning? I'll hear about it forever."

•

With their take-charge, paternalistic attitudes, managers often do very well in their careers but tend to run into difficulty with fellow workers. Other people's "interference" in their carefully thought-out plans is a source of great frustration to them, which is why they usually function better as bosses than underlings.

•

Jay's parents ran a hardware store in Oregon where all family activity and communication took place and the children helped out after school. Dad took care of customers, Mom was at the phone ordering supplies, Jane was positioned at the cash register, Aunt Evelyn kept the books, Ed, the youngest child, did the sweeping and the cleaning, while Jay, the oldest sibling of the three, was at the counter overseeing everything. Mom and Dad enjoyed watching Jay run the show.

Jay devoted his life to the business and by the age of 21 took over when his parents moved to Florida. Ed and Jane soon left the store for new careers. With his troops deserting him, Jay married a hard-working woman accustomed from childhood to criticism and abuse, and before long, they and their children were duplicating the pattern of his youth, all of them centering their lives on the store.

Jay made all the decisions about who went where, who wore what, who did what, who had what, and when everything took place. Not limiting his control to his immediate family, he took care of his in-laws. He supported his parents in Florida, handled his widowed aunt's estate, gave jobs to his brother and sister when they needed them. And he took in a partner who followed orders.

Jay had it made. He ruled over all he surveyed—until everything went wrong. His wife was hospitalized many times for cervical cancer, his children disappointed him, his partner retired, Ed and Jane moved elsewhere. Jay decided he could go it alone without his family and hired outside help. Finally, he divorced his devoted but sickly wife and married a younger woman.

But his new wife soon left him, taking a good portion of his capital. The business fell apart because the hired hands would not tolerate his dictatorial manner, his children stopped speaking to him, he developed heart palpitations, and his debts overwhelmed him. Now a salesman, unable to understand why his formerly successful and familiar role of manager went awry, Jay has just started therapy. He is only beginning to see the part he has played in his own destruction and to understand that he must modify the rigid role he has lived by.

The Family Hero

This is the Super Kid, the Star, the Prima Donna, often the eldest child, who is an overachiever from the start and usually ends up successful and admired by the rest of the family. Even when the Super Kid fails, the family tends to interpret his stumbles in the best possible light, playing down the accomplishments of the others to keep his stardom firmly in place.

Family heroes, always revered though perhaps fiercely resented by their siblings, have been assigned to fulfill the aspirations and unresolved issues of their parents. Their role is to *win*, to shine, to make everyone proud. Therefore, their needs come first in the family and they receive special attention and treatment.

•

Dan prepared his own breakfast and set off for school by himself from the time he entered second grade because at 5 a.m. every morning his mother drove his brother, Bruce, star of the swimming team and the household, to a pool half an hour away for practice, waited for him, then dropped him off at school by 8. Like most siblings of family heroes, Dan never questioned the unusual treatment Bruce received because, of course, he recognized that his brother was special. Nevertheless, his self-esteem suffered from the knowledge that he came second.

•

As a result of the pressure placed firmly upon them and the favoritism they have come to expect, family heroes usually grow up to be highly ambitious, competitive, goal-oriented, forceful people who are not easily distracted by other people's problems. They focus on their goals to the exclusion of all else.

People cast in the role of family hero tend to be narcissistic, seeing themselves through other people's eyes and basking in their own reflection. This means their concept of self is always in flux. Pauline put it this way: "When I didn't get an 'A' in school, I was nothing, a total nobody. When I got one, I was everything, the greatest."

•

Vivian loves being the star wherever she goes. "I know I live for the respect and the applause. They are what turn me on. Competition is in my blood. I can't understand how anyone can tolerate being mediocre and I will work my head off to excel. Isn't that what life is all about?" A championship figure skater, Vivian is heading for the top, without question. "Being Number One is who I am," she says. "Why would anyone settle for less?"

•

It's not that prima donnas are unsympathetic to other people, merely that they don't think about them very much. For this reason, heroes are often lonely people. They, like managers, frequently have a hard time achieving closeness with others and find themselves in superficial relationships where the most important element is how well their own needs are met.

Among the siblings, the family heroes are the ones most likely to be three thousand miles away when family crises occur, leaving their brother or sister to cope. They are the siblings who fly in for a day or two when absolutely necessary and then everyone else is delighted and impressed with them. Look how they've taken time out of their busy schedules to care about the family!

•

Bernice recalls, "I wanted to be there for Mother. I wanted to spend time with her when she was sick, but I was studying for exams and I couldn't get away. Besides, I knew my sister would handle everything, and she did. Kate is a wonderful sister. She's the one who's been taking care of Mother and Pop these last years and she's so good with them. But then, she's not under the same kind of pressure I am. She's married, has kids, lives in the next town to my parents, and doesn't have to worry about making her own living. They all understand how busy I am. I get there when I can."

•

Driven by competition, heroes expect to do well and often succeed. On the other hand, they tend to be vulnerable and insecure, always fearful of failure. Therefore they do not cope well with setbacks en route to their goals, and tend to be subject to depression and anxiety. Their need to achieve drives them to become workaholics who may take unnecessary risks.

Stars tend to pick mates who cater to them. Then they become dependent on them and their servitude, often belittling them and trying to keep them in the background. Imagine their horror if they find out that they have married "the mouse that roared," someone who eventually has enough of such treatment and leaves. When rejected, their pattern is to go through a brief but profound period of loss before finding a replacement and moving right on.

The Forgotten Sibling (a.k.a., Odd Man Out)

Lost in the crowd, forgotten siblings are loners, quiet and withdrawn, people who learned at an early age not to rock the boat.

Usually middle children or among the last of a large number of siblings who have pretty much brought themselves up, or the sibling who has grown up with a star, they grow up feeling overlooked and left out of the mainstream of the family. Their parents, who may be devoted to their older or younger siblings, have assigned them the role of staying out of the way and making no waves. As a result, they feel unimportant and unnoticed. As adults, they usually try to pass through life quietly and unobtrusively.

•

"I've always felt invisible," says Ginger. "I was never noticed except when I really misbehaved and then everyone was amazed because that wasn't like me. My two sisters didn't seem to have the same problem. From my point of view, they got plenty of attention. I remember one day I got dressed for school and purposely put on two different shoes, one black and one white, just to see what would happen. Nobody noticed until I got to school. I felt like I never really existed, until I met my husband who has finally made me feel as if I matter."

•

Whatever forgotten children do, they get little notice. They are never given much responsibility and no great expectations are ever placed on them. They are often the siblings who separate from the family, move to the other side of the country, and are rarely thought of again. As one man said when a childhood friend asked for a report on his family, "Oh, my brother Bobby. He lives in Wisconsin. We haven't seen him in twenty years. Send him Christmas cards every year, but we didn't make it out to his wedding."

•

Tiffany, who was brought up to be the star, had a sister, Diane, who was a forgotten child. And like most who have come to accept this role, Diane is competent, capable, and contained. "I grew up in Tiffany's shadow," she says, "and I've always been jealous of her because she got the major attention in our house. But, to tell the truth, I don't like pressure anyway. The limelight makes me very uncomfortable." Diane goes on, "My boss tells me I'm his best worker and he doesn't understand why I never ask for a raise or a promotion." She admits, "Actually, I like being the one who isn't always expected to be wonderful. Maybe it's because I'm used to it, but I'm more comfortable this way."

•

People who are cast as the overlooked siblings tend to be excellent employees, who take pride in doing their jobs efficiently and correctly. And slowly but surely, they manage to get where they want to go.

Finding mates is not too difficult for these siblings because they are relatively undemanding. Because they are gentle and giving, consistent, unobtrusive, and easy to get along with, they make perfect partners for stars who are not eager to share the limelight.

•

Diane, for example, married a man much like her sister, Tiffany. "Socializing has always been difficult for me—I could never think of anything to say to people. Mike is so charming and dynamic that everyone is drawn to him and I don't have to do much to be accepted but let him carry the conversation. When we go someplace together, I don't have to worry because he makes it easy for me."

•

Most forgotten siblings are good at making and keeping friends, again because they tend to be agreeable and undemanding, seldom criticizing or imposing. However, in most cases, their own needs are not adequately met by others, so they tend to be at the mercy of chance happenings. If, like Diane, they are lucky and their attributes are discovered and valued, they fare well. If not, they may drift by, unnoticed and unappreciated. Worse, their low self-esteem often makes them subject to the needs and wants of other people and they are the ones who are most likely to be abused or abandoned.

The Rebel

These family members take center stage by causing a ruckus. Making up their own rules as they go along, rebels—often charming, glittery, and intriguing—have assumed the role of taking the attention off other family problems. Rebels are constantly testing the boundaries of the family and are responsible for bringing home new ideas and new ways of doing things.

•

Jack is 25 years old and has no problem admitting that his role in the family is to be the one who refuses to abide by the rules. He was the second youngest. His younger brother was the family pet; an older brother, the eldest child, was the hero; an older sister played the caretaker, and his next older sister, the manager. He knows each of their roles perfectly and says, "If I had to do it over again, I wouldn't change a thing."

Jack battled with his father, a highly respected Rabbi in the orthodox community who, from as early as he can remember, was relentlessly dominating. Jack was told by his mother that he was her favorite and he suspected it was because he confronted his father when no one else, especially Mom, had the courage. "It always took the wind out of his sails when I bucked him because he couldn't do a thing about it. I really shocked him when I moved out after high school and became a body guard for a star. I loved to tell him wild stories about the star's escapades, because he was so wonderfully horrified."

Jack became addicted to both alcohol and drugs before he left his star-studded days behind and came home, after his mother's sudden death, to become a Muslim, a major departure from his Orthodox Jewish upbringing.

He still has not come to terms with the dysfunctional nature of his need to rebel, although he is working hard to do so. He still tends to go to extremes, most of them self-destructive as well as anathema to his father. He is a blue-collar worker in the construction business, while his brothers and sisters all belong to the corporate world. He makes good money but is a compulsive spender who has piled up debts far beyond his control. Meanwhile, he continues to proselytize for his religious group.

•

At the functional end of the rebel spectrum are those who are simply "little devils" who grow up flouting conventional behavior and doing as they please, while everyone else is charmed. Savoring the attention they receive, they will do anything to hold the floor, love to play jokes, and are apt to engage in thoroughly outrageous behavior that the others usually find entertaining. Always doing something surprising, they may make monstrous waves but they rarely self-destruct.

•

The only way Bill felt he had distinction as the youngest of three siblings was to be the cutup, the cute little fellow who destroyed his brother's toys as a joke, and shattered his sister's control over him by keeping her off balance.

"I used to torment my sister by provoking her to hit me and then tattling on her. I remember standing in front of the house when I was about five. I had discovered the fine art of spitting and I was aiming at my sister. A friend of hers said, 'If that was my little brother, I'd slap him right across the face.' So my sister promptly slapped me. I started screaming. She got scared and said, 'I'll buy you some candy if you don't tell Ma.' I took the bribe and then, before I was two steps inside the door, I told on her. I felt bad but it was more important for me to prove that I was in control."

•

At the extreme end of the scale, the rebels are cast as the family troublemakers, getting an inordinately large portion of the group's attention because of their negative behavior. Sometimes they are the scapegoats, who are made to feel at fault for all of the family woes. They are the ones about whom parents feel free to say, "If it weren't for this child, everything would have been wonderful!" and the ones their brothers or sisters can point at and say, "Look what he did!" Classic scapegoats receive no latitude for mistakes. Whatever they do is considered reprehensible. But they do reap their rewards—a sense of power because of their ability to cause such chaos, plenty of attention, and freedom from the obligations of high expectations.

Although they may appear otherwise under their couldn't-careless exteriors, rebel/troublemakers on the extreme end of the spectrum are not happy people. They perform with bravado and act as if they feel nothing but disdain for other people's feelings. But in reality, they feel rejected, totally inadequate, and responsible for the unhappiness they seem to cause others.

Most family rebels fall somewhere in the middle of the spectrum. They are the ones who act out at home, in school, and, later, on the job and in their marriages, in an effort to gain attention. They shun advice from their more establishment siblings and tend to be susceptible to "the wrong kind" of peer pressure. Often uniting the rest of the family in mutual commiseration about their antics, the rebels are proud of their ability to compete on their own terms. Their siblings benefit by looking good in comparison with them and, at the same time, they often secretly envy the rebel's ability to "get away with everything." Rebels of all varieties are not held to the same standards as everyone else and so, in truth, they *do* get away with behavior that others cannot. As a result, they have more freedom to experiment, pursue radical ideas, and come up with new perspectives.

Rebels, especially those who lean toward being scapegoats, often have difficulty with relationships because they are acutely sensitive to rejection and are slow to recoup in their own eyes when they fail. Because they assume they are the bad ones in the relationship, they often find mates who help them fulfill this prophecy, people who encourage their unacceptable behavior and then blame them for it. At the same time, they cast their partners into the role of accuser, whom they enjoy betraying by bad behavior. Mates of rebels do best when they are firm but sensitive to their partner's need for reassurance and love.

The Family Pet

Family pets, usually youngest or only children, are the cuddly teddybears, the babies, the mascots of the family, whom everybody wants to hug and protect. Their role is to dispel tension with charm and humor. They work hard and fast to be the center of attention and tend to doubt their self-worth unless the whole world notices and approves of them. Even as adults, they may panic when asked to do something all by themselves, because they are accustomed to helping hands.

They can be extremely demanding; then again, they truly appreciate what is done for them and tend to express their gratitude freely. In fact, in their case, flattery often gets them everywhere. Other people enjoy being with them because they are warm and engaging and make those around them feel important, worthwhile, superior, and noble—all at the same time. Caretakers, who don't feel they exist unless they have someone to care for, find near-perfect companions in family pets, who need to be tended to and protected.

•

Today, Jesse is 45 years old, a man who only three years ago stopped using cocaine to cope with every situation that would have led him to become an independent adult. Until then, his coke, his elderly parents, his caretaking wife, and everyone else he could find, kept him afloat. His parents were older, scraping by in a small town in Oklahoma and so poor that their first son, thirteen years older than Jesse, had been sent to live with his grandparents. Jesse was born at the right time. The rights to drill their land for oil were leased to a large company and the family prospered. Jesse's mother, who felt they had not properly provided for their elder son, spent the rest of her life catering to her baby.

Jesse never stopped expecting the same treatment everywhere he went. He got jobs that he promptly lost because of absenteeism, only to be rescued by his parents, who sent money and airplane tickets home. The pattern was repeated in his marriage. Jesse married a woman, an only child, who was just as supportive of his self-indulgent behavior as his parents were, even commiserating with him about the "abuse" he had to take at work.

It wasn't until all of his caretakers began to fail him that Jesse realized that he had to make changes in his behavior. His parents died, his wife threatened divorce, his health was failing, and Jesse had to face taking care of himself. In a panic, he joined a substance-abuse therapy group and Cocaine Anonymous. He appears to have made major changes, but at the same time, he has managed to turn some members of the group into his caretakers. Just like everyone else, Jesse is consistent: He will always fall back on his accustomed mode of helplessness and view other people as his saviors, because getting people to take care of him is the role he knows best. At the same time, by becoming aware of what he is doing, he is working on constructing a healthier version of his dependent personality.

•

People who play the role of family pet are anxious to please. They are attentive and sympathetic and do their best to make the others feel good by asking for advice, help, or instruction. But they pay a price for their dependence. Constantly attuned to stress and conflict but usually unaware of the source, they are often high-strung, nervous, and hyperactive. They are often riddled with inferiority complexes, feeling unworthy and incapable in the face of competition. Family pets can be resentful, too, that they are not considered capable of taking care of themselves.

The Special Sibling

The siblings who suffer from physical or mental handicaps so disabling that they become the focus of the entire family occupy very important roles because they often end up with tremendous power over the other siblings. When their needs dominate the entire group, these less-fortunate children may turn into tyrants, a situation that limits them and, at the same time, makes their brothers or sisters feel neglected.

•

Richard was such a child. Totally incapacitated by cerebral palsy, he was unable even to feed himself and could communicate in sounds intelligible only to his mother and older sister. He dominated his family, however, and could easily be termed the most powerful sibling in the house. His sister and brother, highly intelligent, were given credit only when they attended to him, and their high marks in school were both expected and ignored.

Although Richard died at the age of 29, twenty years ago, his siblings still suffer from an inability to enjoy themselves without guilt. After all, how could they have a good time when Richard spent his life trapped in his terrifyingly dysfunctional body?

•

Special siblings help to define and magnify the roles of all the others. Caretakers, for example, sharpen their skills caring for their needs. Family clowns learn to use their humor to relieve the tension rampant in the household. Heroes work hard to try to compensate their parents for their sibling's deficiencies.

But no matter what special siblings do, they always win. Because of their limitations, the family expectations for them are minimal and their most minor accomplishments are applauded as great victories. Manipulative and competitive as they may be—and many special siblings are extremely manipulative, since their maladies give them great power—they are tolerated and accepted because the others feel it is not right to oppose them. In this case, birth order is not relevant. Sibling rivalry is not relevant. When you have a profoundly retarded sister, it doesn't matter whether she is the oldest or the youngest, you can't compete with her because you can't win.

Just as it is not permitted to defeat or even compete against a severely disabled brother or sister, it is not permissible to resent him either. After all, you are the lucky one. Since Johnny is confined to a wheelchair, how can you resent him just because you have to take him for a walk every afternoon?

•

When Carl, age 9, complained to his mother when he didn't get permission to invite a friend to sleep over, she exclaimed, "How can you talk like that? Sarah has never had a good day in her life!" Sarah, eight years his senior, had been born with severe heart defects that kept her confined to the house. Not only was it unacceptable for Carl to enjoy himself, he wasn't permitted to complain either.

•

Stan faced similar problems growing up in the shadow of his brother who, as a toddler, had been severely scalded and for years thereafter underwent a series of reconstructive surgeries. Although an exceptionally talented boy, Stan was allowed very few moments on center stage. Worse yet, he was expected to understand that his mother was busy with more important matters. To this day, Stan feels emasculated and inferior to his brother, who has gone on to become a successful accountant, husband, and father, while Stan continues to search for his place in life.

•

Very often, special siblings understand the untenable positions in which their problems place their families. But while they may regret it, they tend to use their power over their siblings to their own advantage because it may be their only path to even a little control and a sense of momentary superiority. It's hard to blame a special sibling for using any tactic at his disposal, because there is no denying that he has not had the same advantages as the others.

•

In our waiting room, Betsy had no problem maneuvering her wheelchair around the furniture to get a glass of water from the cooler. But when it was time for her first interview, in her anxiety she bumped into the front desk and the doors, and was finally propelled by helpful hands. Without realizing it then, she was playing on everyone's sympathies, having learned that looking helpless could bring positive rewards.

Afflicted by a progressive disease of the peripheral nervous system, Betsy, now 27, was suffering from severe depression. When she came to us for counseling, she talked about her younger brother, Jay, who had just received a scholarship to a distant university, but she was very hesitant to discuss her true feelings toward him. As she became more comfortable in therapy, it began to be obvious that her feelings were mixed.

"He's trying to decide whether to accept the scholarship, because it means he has to leave me behind. He is a great brother. He's always there to take care of me and spend time with me. But Jay is whole and I am not. He can have a life and I cannot. I hate him because he has it all. And now he's probably going to leave me, and I can't stand it."

Betsy was desperate for control. Controlling Jay and her parents with her helplessness was her way of feeling powerful, even though she hated using it as a tool. Luckily for all of them, she eventually accepted the fact that she had to make a life for herself and release Jay from eternal bondage. She became involved in her own progress toward a career in computer programming and now takes satisfaction in her ability to live in her own apartment with the help of an aide.

Making Adjustments

If you keep in mind that you and your siblings will each see things from your own unique points of view, none of them necessarily reflecting total reality, you will be less surprised when you run into strong resistance as you try to change familiar patterns. Your siblings are not maliciously blocking you, nor do they wish to cause you unhappiness. They, like most people, are merely striving to keep things just the way they are. After all, that's what they know and that's what feels most comfortable for them—and for you as well.

But when the roles that you assumed in your early days and have carried over into the rest of your life become burdensome, disadvantageous, or downright dysfunctional, it is time to make modifications, whether or not you have the cooperation of the rest of the family. Simply by understanding and acknowledging that you never stray far from your traditional role—especially when you feel uncertain, whether at home, in the office, or out on a date—you have already started to make a change. Awareness is the first step to seeing things differently. You can't make yourself over into somebody else, nor should you; but now you can start redefining yourself and, in the process, translating your role into healthier expressions.

But first, it's important to recognize that, based on your labels and your accustomed role, you have developed your own special way of fighting off perceived threats to your territorial rights and your self-esteem. Originally designed to protect your fragile ego against the assaults of your siblings, these self-protective techniques are the weapons you will always pull out first when you are fighting for control.

7

Psychological Warfare: The Tactics Siblings Use

Joe is 52 years old and still ends up in a rage whenever he speaks to his sister on the telephone. "I can't talk to her for more than two minutes," he says, "before I'm ready to tell her off. She keeps letting me know in one way or another that I'm not doing enough for Mom. I never visit, I never call her up, I'm never available to do her errands. My sister feels she has to do everything. That's ridiculous! I do all I can for my mother. I love my mother. I send her money every month, I make sure to call her at least once a week, and I get to see her when I can. I'm a busy man, I've got a family and a business, and I live two hundred miles away. My sister has a family, she works, but she lives in the next town and she's the kind of person who likes to take over. That's always been her job and that's fine, just don't bug me."

Joe's problem is that he's been set up by his older caretaker sister once again. She knows exactly how to get to him. What's more, he knows exactly how to get to her by brushing off what she thinks is important. "When I say, 'Sis, that's enough, I don't want to hear another word about it,' she goes crazy. Actually, although I know Marian would do anything in the world for me if I needed her, I see and talk to her only when I have to. I leave it up to my wife to make the obligatory calls."

•

Joe is engaged in psychological warfare with his sister, warfare that has been going on between them since they were children. Marian, the eldest, was always in charge, taking care of Joe but also making sure he behaved himself according to her standards. Her tactic, although she has always loved him and probably isn't consciously aware of how she behaves with him, has been to make him feel guilty when he doesn't perform. She does this by making him feel he should always be doing more for his family. And it's never enough.

His weapon against her attack is rejection. When she lays on the guilt, he cuts her off and refuses to discuss the subject—or anything else, for that matter. Joe played the role of family star and has always understood on some unconscious level that his family considers his attention, words, gifts, to be manna from heaven. So he withholds them when Marian tries to overpower him, and then she feels deprived of his grace. As a result, she is more compelled to control him, trying even harder to make him do his part. And he moves farther away.

Since it doesn't produce the results she's after, why doesn't Marian change her tactics? Because she can't. She is so accustomed to dealing with her younger brother in this way that merely hearing his voice puts her on "automatic pilot." Always unconsciously fearful that he will abandon her, she tries to pull him back, reverting to the method she has perfected. She knows from past history that if she keeps on making him feel guilty, he will eventually be unable to resist the pressure. He always has.

Finally, Marian's tactic allows her to feel a sense of superiority. By demanding that Joe do the "right" thing, such as remembering to call his mother on her birthday, she continues to play her traditional role of the good sister, the good daughter, the caretaker, the family member who anticipates their mother's needs and makes sure her brother does his part too.

And Joe? First feeling like the bad son and an inadequate person when his sister proclaims he is not living up to her expectations, he then gains a sense of control and importance when he walks away, refusing to listen and making her pursue him. He knows she will come after him, which, in truth, he welcomes because in his heart he wants to feel he is a needed and important member of the family. Around and around they go. Joe says, "The worst part is that, although we really love each other and we are both good people, we never feel good for long, no matter what we do, and we always part with an ugly feeling. We can't seem to break the cycle."

Learning to Protect Yourself

To survive psychologically, you must feel good—at least to some degree and in some ways—about yourself. You must feel that you excel somewhere, somehow; that you are *somebody*, a person of substance to whom attention must be paid. You need to feel, as does everyone else, that you have some power over your environment. Put another way, you *don't* want to be the loser in any relationship. You *don't* want to feel inadequate, unwanted, unworthy, or unacceptable. At all costs, you try not to feel inferior.

So from the time you are born, you start developing your own style of safeguarding yourself, your technique of controlling the forces around you, designed to keep you believing that you are equal to or maybe better than other people. First by instinct and later through unconscious interaction with your parents and siblings and the other players in your life, you refine, alter, and practice your techniques until finally you have invented a pattern of presentation, a way of exhibiting yourself to the world that is identifiable, unique, and remarkably predictable. It includes the barrier you erect as a shield against intrusion by people who want to know more about you than you want them to know, and also a set of probes or missiles that you deploy to explore unknown territory and deflect any threats you perceive to be aimed at your self-respect.

Serving your needs for security and acceptance, these tactics help preserve your image, protect your positions, and give you a sense of superiority. They make you feel you are in control of your world and safeguarded against expectations you feel you can't handle. In the process, unfortunately, it often means you make others look bad so you can look good.

Always on Alert

Although everybody engages in psychological warfare, it is with our siblings that we develop our techniques, refining them to perfection, and keeping them always at hand ready to be activated. Eventually they become so much a part of us that, most of the time, we don't even know we are using them.

This doesn't mean that we are always at war. Much of the time, with our siblings as well as with other people, we can genuinely enjoy one another, get along well, and feel reasonably secure. It is only when our positions are threatened, when we feel we are not getting our fair share and are in danger of being the loser, when we feel inadequate and inferior, that the jockeying begins and our weapons are fired.

The major clue, the directional signal that points to the rivalry between any two people, is defensiveness. When you feel vulnerable, unprepared, uneasy, you prepare to fight. Consciously or unconsciously, you feel you must protect yourself against attack or exposure of your inadequacies and insecurities. What you are really defending are your deepest doubts about yourself.

The mechanisms you invent to protect yourself are absolutely normal, useful, and in most cases healthy. They are an important part of your coping skills. None of us could survive without them, because we all have our soft spots that we don't want exposed or exploited and we all want to feel we have control over our lives.

The tactics you customarily utilize when you feel defensive form a pattern of behavior that bears your own personal stamp. You'll continue to use the same ones all your life, perhaps with a few inventive variations on tap to fit the circumstances.

Perhaps, for example, you feel that you are "an impostor," someone who has attained his present status by accident. You were not chosen to be vice president because of your intelligence or talent, but because you were persistent or lucky. Your secret fear is that you will be found out. You don't want other people to discover that you are an inadequate person who doesn't deserve much credit for your accomplishments. You'll protect that vulnerability by using your defensive weapons at the first indication that you may be seen as not all that intelligent or talented.

Siblings Set You Up

Your siblings can usually trigger your tactical stance quicker than anyone else. After all, who knows your well-protected secrets better than they? In fact, they are experts at setting you up. Maybe they don't call you back when you've left a message. Maybe they say in a critical tone, "Don't get temperamental on us," when you are known as "the emotional one" in the family. Or perhaps your brother starts talking about something else in the middle of your story about your harrowing trip to the airport, and you feel a lack of respect, just as you did when you were kids.

Sometimes it's nothing more than a look or a rolling of the eyes when you make a statement you think is important. Or a paternal pat on the head. Sometimes it's an offer of help that you don't want or need but must express gratitude for. Often it's what they *don't* say, a feeling that you are being ignored or minimized. It can be a back-handed compliment or an emotional stance that makes you feel trapped.

•

Arthur's most powerful feeling of vulnerability is his fear of social ineptitude and unacceptability. The youngest of three brothers, he has always felt slower and less capable than Larry and Saul, four and five years his senior, who were extremely intelligent, articulate, and seemingly supremely self-confident. As a child, Arthur played the part of the little hanger-on who was ready to perform any service for his brothers to gain their favor and the pleasure of their company. Today, at 37, he continues to feel that his relationships are tenuous and dependent on the services he constantly offers other people.

An enthusiastic sailor, he recently decided to join a boat club. When he was accepted, he was elated and called Larry to tell him the good news. "Gee," Larry exclaimed, "why did you join *that* club? They'll take anybody. You want to join the Island Boat Club. That's the one that counts. Hey, it just occurs to me—I know the commodore. I'll give him a call and put in a good word for you."

Zap! In one quick interchange, Larry demoralized Arthur. Arthur's acceptance into the club had been turned into a foolish mistake and Larry had proved his superiority by knowing a more important club as well as more important people. He infantilized his younger brother, just as he always had, to keep Arthur in an inferior position and, at the same time, aggrandize himself. Why? Perhaps he felt threatened by his brother's unaccustomed independent move and his intrusion into his own special territory—popularity, social savvy, and the right contacts.

Arthur had learned early in life that if he was going to carve out a niche in the family, his options were limited. His two older, more powerful, and controlling brothers put him, along with the dog, into the role of the family pet who needed their help to survive. So he tolerated the indignities and the putdowns he received and tried to seem grateful for their "help." As you will soon see, Arthur's own protective mechanism was the Goody Two-Shoes Tactic.

Don't Take It Personally

Since our maneuvers serve a dual purpose, they should not be viewed in terms of good or bad but, rather, in terms of how well they do the job of helping us navigate and function. Their first purpose is to protect the tender sense of self; the second is to control outsiders and limit their power over us. This can be accomplished by elevating ourselves or by belittling them, if only in our own minds, or by a combination of the two.

Because family relationships are always dynamic, the war between siblings never ends in absolute victory or total defeat. Winning is usually short-lived and the rewards ephemeral. Nor will any of us ever lay down our defensive weaponry and ego-elevating devices for long. Although we may learn new ones or train ourselves to use the old ones more sparingly and less hurtfully, they have become our standard ways of dealing with life's problems. They are a permanent part of our personalities.

As a result, we are all amazingly predictable, one good reason why siblings feel comfortable, if not always happy, with one another. Although we may not be consciously aware of it, we know our own style, we know our siblings' style, and we all know exactly what to expect and how far we can go.

Joe's sister, Marian, for example, whom we encountered at the beginning of this chapter, will surely use the same "guilting" technique wherever she goes. When she feels rejected, overburdened, unfairly treated, unappreciated, uncertain, she will try to make others feel they are not carrying their full load. Joe expects it and would be amazed and disconcerted if she changed her tactics. He, for his part, has perfected his disappearing act and will always tend to gain the upper hand by using rejection as his weapon. Marian expects it. Even his employees have learned to count on his stony expression when they overstep their boundaries, and his wife may get annoyed but is not at all surprised when he tunes her out.

What's Your Style?

The following are some of the most common protective mechanisms. You'll be sure to recognize the ones you and your siblings use on each other, the familiar patterns that elicit predictable responses. Although you may, at one time or another, make use of several of the tactics, one of them undoubtedly serves as your first line of defense.

Because these techniques are always triggered by feelings of vulnerability, they point directly at your core issues—those areas where, because they are the most important to your self-image, you feel most easily threatened—often masking disabling inferiorities. Sometimes they don't work the way you want them to and, instead elicit such negative responses that they become your greatest deterrent to realizing the goals you are trying to achieve when you use them.

Once you recognize your usual tactics (if you can't figure them out, ask your brother or sister!), you can then decide whether they help or hinder you in your relationships with other people, and whether you want to try to modify them. You will also surely detect the typical defensive patterns of each of your siblings and how they are used on you. A bonus: you may be pleasantly surprised, as you work through your problems with your siblings and come to know yourself and them better, that you don't feel so vulnerable to them and will become more flexible. Therefore you won't need to rely so heavily on those same old tactics.

The Guilting Gambit

This works when it's used on you because, like everyone else, you want to think of yourself as a good person, and you are being made to feel that you are not. If your brother or sister uses this technique, then he or she is telling you that you haven't done enough. If *you* are using this technique, then you are doing your best to make your sibling feel inferior to you, a wonderful, hardworking, giving individual.

Marian is a master at using this device, and it gets to her brother, Joe, every time. Overwhelmed by the responsibility of her mother and yet unable to step out of her role as caretaker, Marian defends her role by highlighting Joe's deficits when he attempts to help. At the same time, she feels superior to him because she's the one who knows what Mother really needs. Although she resents the burden of caring for her, she ends up feeling smarter and more competent than her brother, the exalted family hero, and, in the process, forces him to perform, thereby subjugating him to her.

If he eludes her control and doesn't respond, but runs away instead, then he looks bad because he seems to have abandoned his mother in her time of need. All this has been accomplished by the clever use of guilt.

The Rejection Ruse

One of the most powerful weapons you can use against another person who threatens your position is to reject him or ignore him, acting as though you don't hear him or as though he is not important enough to warrant your attention.

Although it's a technique sometimes employed by middles and youngests who don't dare fight back overtly, this tactic is most often used by an older sibling whose resentment at having been dethroned by a younger one carries over into later life. It can play itself out in the typical childhood scenario of the younger sibling tagging along with the big kids, being ignored or even chased away, left out of all the fun. The message from the bigger sibling is "You don't belong here, so just go away!"

The use of rejection is usually based on the pecking order, with the dominant sibling employing it against the weaker one who is more dependent upon family attachments. But it is also effective when employed by a sibling to deflect the intimidation of a more powerful brother or sister, rendering the intimidation and the person using it less potent. It delivers the message "Do whatever you want. Throw your weight around. I don't care. I am not affected in the least."

In Joe's case, he lets Marian do the day-to-day work for their mother, thereby giving himself the freedom to live his life as the star. When she threatens his role by pointing out his failings, he fends her off by rejecting her, minimizing her importance, and remaining firmly on his pedestal. This allows *him* to feel superior and in control of her.

Rejection may also be used to keep you out of already claimed territory or to make you perform as you "should." It can be subtle, such as forgetting your birthday or not quite making it to your anniversary party. Perhaps it's never calling so that you must always initiate the contact in order to stay in touch. Or maybe it's responding, when you say you'd like to come to visit, with "I'm really sorry but I just won't have time. I have so many important appointments."

•

Gwen's two sisters, more than a dozen years older than herself, played the role of surrogate mothers and doted on her throughout her childhood. But when she got married at 19 without their approval, they responded by acting as though they'd lost all interest in her and what she did with her life. She had carried her independence too far and, in addition, she threatened the family ethos of social acceptability by marrying the wrong kind of man. For years they kept their distance, hurt, angry and resentful, rarely speaking with her, inviting her only to major family functions, and finding many excuses for not attending her important occasions.

Gwen had married an affluent self-made man twelve years her senior. Her sisters expressed their disapproval of his earlier divorce and his ostentatious life style, making her feel they were embarrassed by his lack of culture and taste. "But when I was getting a divorce from Roy, they really rallied around and were a tremendous support for me," Gwen says. "I guess they were right about him all along and I knew it. It wasn't long before I began to recognize all the faults they saw in him and wonder why I'd made such a stupid mistake."

Upon analysis, it appeared that Gwen's marriage to Roy had seriously threatened her sisters' control over her. Their helpless little sister had found a new caretaker, an older, rich husband. So they did just as they had always done when they were all much younger: They rejected her. And ultimately they won. When Gwen broke off with her husband, she returned to the fold and her role as the family pet who needed all the help she could get.

The Goody Two-Shoes Tactic

Always the child in the family who feels the least loved, the practitioner of the Goody Two-Shoes Tactic feels that she *must* be good, because nothing else will be tolerated, and if she doesn't perform, she will be cast out.

•

Marvin is the youngest in his family, but he is the designated caretaker as well as the "good one," who has always assumed responsibility for his parents and, until she died recently, his grandmother. His two older sisters and one brother left home long ago to get married and establish themselves in other communities, but Marvin, now 38, has put his life on hold. Good-looking, intelligent, and successful in his job in a large corporation, he lives at home, where he does everything from mowing the lawn to shopping for groceries and making repairs.

An extremely anxious person whose primary fears are rejection and disapproval, Marvin has finally decided that he must move into his own apartment if he is ever to establish his identity. At the same time, he is intensely concerned about upsetting his family, who count on him to hold things together. To him, not being good is being bad. His brother and sisters feel the same way—for him, not for them.

When he tentatively announced that he was looking for an apartment, there was a flurry of telephone calls among his siblings, who came over to the house one Sunday afternoon ostensibly to visit their parents.

"Sure," said his sibling of significance, his brother who is his next-older sibling, "you should move out, but this is a bad time to do it. You should wait till Dad's feeling better and Mom isn't so upset about Grandma." To top it off, his sister told a mutual friend to tell Marvin that his father was looking poorly. After this sibling visit, Marvin felt even more uncertain about the wisdom of making a change.

•

Being good has its flip side. The sibling who uses it as a maneuver is saying to his potential critics, "Look how good I am and how bad you are, only thinking about yourselves." Or "Don't worry about me. I'll stay home and take care of Mom and Dad. You go on out and have fun." This was the way Marvin made himself feel superior to his siblings and strengthened himself against their subjugation of him. He made his SOS—his brother—feel calculating and materialistic compared to him. He was the saint and his brother the sinner. Not only that, but Marvin used his parents' needs as an excuse for not taking on the risks of living his own life. As long as he played this game, he did not have to assume the responsibilities of being a grownup on his own. He learned this technique early. He remembers that as a child he would stay home and bake with his mom instead of going to the park with the other kids. When his siblings went out to play too, he let them know they should feel bad for not helping Mom.

•

Arthur, the man who joined the "wrong" boat club, also secretly believed that he was a far better person than his two older brothers because he was always there for them, ready to help them out. He played the two brothers against each other, keeping them off balance and in competition by telling one, when asked to do something for him, that he was too busy helping the other. The more the brothers relied upon him for services, the more powerful he felt. And the more he could avoid concentrating on his failing marriage and lackluster career.

The Infantilization Device

The object of this tactic, most often played by the older of two siblings, is to treat a brother or sister like an incompetent child: "Let me help you, you'll never be able to do it yourself."

•

Take, for example, two brothers who are partners in a furniture store. Frank, the older one, manages to get his message across every day with remarks like "I'll handle the customers because I know how to talk to them. You were never good with people. It's best if you stay in the office and take care of the books."

In only a few words, he has diminished his brother and elevated himself and, at the same time, has emerged like the good guy who is looking after his kid brother.

•

Infantilizing the competition is a powerful technique that makes the other person feel small, stupid, and inadequate, feelings that hardly bring joy to anyone's heart. The only defense to this insidious maneuver is to insist that you certainly can take care of yourself. The problem is that, after long years of being its recipient, you may have come to believe that you genuinely can't stand on your own two feet.

Larry, who extinguished his brother Arthur's exuberance about acceptance by the boat club, was using this technique to make Arthur feel he couldn't manage his own life without help—help from *him*, the superior being. Arthur lives in fear of alienating Larry, so he tolerates the indignities to which he is subjected, and continues to appear grateful for everything.

The *Mea Culpa* Maneuver

This is one of a number of similar tactics whose goal is to take control by making your sibling feel sorry for you (or you for him). It goes like this: "You're right, I'm wrong. I shouldn't have done it. What's the matter with me? I am so stupid. I don't know what made me do such a dumb thing."

Have you heard this one? It's a customary maneuver from a person who feels he can get away with almost anything as long as he confesses that he's no darned good. The usual response to this defense is forgiveness, with some underlying resentment, however. How can you beat up on someone who is so sorry he has caused you so much trouble?

•

Consider Billy, who crashed his brother's bicycle riding down a steep hill in a race with his pals. "Gee, George, I feel terrible. Look what I did. I'm always doing awful things. I'll work nights, I'll save all my money from now until Christmas, and I'll buy you one just like it."

•

What can you say? After all, this must be a good person because he feels so bad about being bad. "Don't worry about it," you're likely to say, "I don't really need a bicycle anyway. I don't use it much. It's O.K. You didn't mean it."

This is a passive-aggressive pattern that is calculated to make you feel you'd be the cruelest person on earth to blame or punish him. It renders you helpless because you cannot take revenge without looking like an ogre. Worse, you are forced to accept the consequences with a forgiving smile or a feeble platitude.

•

Burton grew up with just such a brother, Sam, who was three years his junior. "I'd get a new suit. Sam would manage to spill grape juice on it by mistake when he was getting a tray ready to serve Mom breakfast in bed. I'd worked on a science project for three months when Sam accidentally crashed into it chasing the dog who was chasing the cat. As best man at my wedding, he managed to lose the wedding bands in the apartment incinerator while he was helping out in the kitchen.

"All of those times, I knew he felt terrible and I knew he couldn't help it. He was always so anxious to please. There was never anything I could do about it. At the same time, I was angry. And I felt vastly superior to him because I didn't screw up like he always did—and like a saint for being able to tolerate the never-ending misfortunes he laid on me. But I always suspected he never did this stuff to his own things, only mine."

Sam, for his part, had his complaints about Burt and managed to feel superior because he considered himself a much better person than his brother:

"Everything has always come easy for Burt but I've had to work very hard for what I've ever got. He's smart, organized, coordinated, and he's lucky. I'm none of the above. Burt's a great guy, don't get me wrong, but he has little tolerance for people's short-comings. I remember when we were teenagers, I hit the garage-door button by mistake and the door came down right in the middle of the hood of his old beat-up car. He accused me of being jealous that he had a car. I told him I would never do something like that on purpose and that I was genuinely sorry. He never said much about it but he has always made me feel like such a jerk. I would never do that to anybody."

•

Serving to disarm the opposition, the *Mea Culpa* Maneuver is a weapon that cunningly neutralizes a perceived greater force, in this case what Sam feels are Burton's superior attributes. It allows its practitioner to avoid direct "hand-to-hand" combat and yet win the battle. It gives him power over his sibling without the fear of retribution and, at the same time, provides a safe outlet for profound resentment over strong feelings of inferiority and envy.

Probably the most difficult self-protective style for a sibling to cope with when performed to perfection, this maneuver provides an opportunity for few counter moves except confrontation and rejection.

The Sickly Syndrome

The Sickly Syndrome similarly employs passive-aggressive techniques. Siblings who use this one as a primary mode of gaining control are usually very anxious people who find life packed with expectations that they cannot hope to fulfill. By inflating any illness to epic proportions, they are proclaiming that they can't be held responsible for their failings. "How can I come to your party when I am feeling so bad?" "Do you really expect me to drive all the way into town to help Dad pack when it's all I can do to get around the house?"

Suffering from ailments ranging from migraines to asthma to ulcers to cardiac arrhythmias to backaches and worse, these people experience actual symptoms, whether their origins are real or imagined, that are the barometers of overloaded systems. Underneath it all, they are perfectionists who cannot readily admit incompetence or a need for help. Their illness gives them a way to get sympathy and assistance without having to ask for it. It is only with great insight that one can see through to their innermost conflicts that are invariably deeply rooted in a fear of failure. Their illnesses excuse them from trying and risking failure. At the same time, they feel no need to apologize for their enslavement of you because, after all, they are sick.

Siblings whose hypochondria excuses them from responsibility are extremely difficult to counter. Although you, on the receiving end, may feel superior because of your comparative strength, you will be the one who must cope with family responsibilities and experience tremendous frustration. Although you may be resentful, it's hard to confront a sickly brother or sister.

•

"When I was growing up," says Mary, "my sister Sally got all the attention. She had a disorder called Tourette's syndrome that made her twitch and grimace and come out with strange sounds that were terrifying and terribly embarrassing to me. She was 5 when I was born and I never remember her being any different.

I remember that the doctors couldn't do anything for her but just said to keep the pressure off her. She was always worse when she got stressed out. Whenever there was tension in the house, Sally would start to twitch and shout things like 'Fuck you!' or 'Eat shit!' Well, needless to say, it was a weird environment to grow up in, but the high hopes that would have been laid on Sally got transferred to me and I received a double dose of the family's expectations."

Mary was a good student but the pressure on her to succeed was intense. "For example, my father used to ask me, when I brought home a 93, if that was the highest mark in the class. He always made me feel I wasn't doing good enough."

Mary remembers that one day she realized she too could get attention like Sally. "I was running down a hill when I was about 6 and suddenly my knee buckled and I fell head over heels. My mother came running, yelling for my father. When I told them I couldn't put weight on my foot, off we went to the hospital where the doctors found nothing wrong. My parents worried until, after about three days, I seemed to be able to walk normally. That was the first time I had ever felt my parents were more concerned about me than Sally."

Mary's pattern from then on has been to blame her failings on her "nerves," complaining about headaches and stomach pains whenever the going gets rough, forcing her family, including Sally, to cater to her. "When my stomach pains got bad, Sally would have to bring me my supper in bed and do my chores for me. Finally her 'Fuck you!' and 'Eat shit!' utterances made sense to me."

It is only now that Mary is beginning to recognize that the purpose of her tactics has been to induce sympathy for her problems and, at the same time, to minimize the expectations her parents had for her. Not much can be asked of someone who is ill.

The Big Baby Tactic

Used mainly by a youngest child or the youngest boy or girl in the family, this one, the flip side of infantilization, evolves when siblings realize that other people will always protect them if they behave like babies. Helpless, defenseless, they can't take care of themselves so others must cater to them, doing anything to make them stop whining, complaining, crying, pouting, stamping their feet, and throwing tantrums.

When your siblings use the Big Baby Tactic, they gain control of the situation, while you feel overwhelmingly like a bad person as you try to defend yourself. The rewards for big babies are enormous: constant attention, nurturing, and power. Their siblings—and anybody else who falls into their trap—can't walk away from them without becoming alienated from the family.

Adults who use the baby defense continue to control others by threatening to go to pieces if they don't get what they want. Babies never let go, always making sure somebody is there to take care of them. Let them down and they punish you by getting into deeper trouble—and it's all your fault.

•

"My sister Jane is so childish," Joe says, "you have to be careful what you say to her. My wife says she always has to play second fiddle to Jane because we're all so afraid of upsetting her. Her feelings get hurt very easily and then she goes away and sulks. She tends to get depressed and lately she's developed a real drinking problem. I end up bailing her out of all kinds of messes although she's probably the smartest of all of us, but she can't seem to get her act together."

•

Usually most successful within the family confines, the Big Baby Tactic can have great disadvantages outside of it. When your only skill is calling for help, you are not likely to make your way in the world. You become a dependent, discouraged person who may feel very important when other people rally around to save you, but you feel like *nothing* when they don't.

The Poor Me Posture

"Poor me," or playing the martyr, is another variation on the theme of controlling others by making them feel sorry for you. It is also quite similar to the Big Baby Tactic.

•

It's a rare week that Sarah doesn't hang up feeling disheartened and a little angry after talking to her younger sister Natalie on the telephone, a weekly custom. She has listened to an endless tale of woe while carefully refraining from telling Natalie anything good about her own life.

"I can't tell Natalie I enjoyed a party last week, that I love my husband, that my kids are behaving just fine, because she makes me feel bad for not being as miserable as she is. I even find myself digging up a few problems to tell her about so things don't sound too good. After all, she's now divorced for the third time, the men she meets all seem great at first but inevitably end up treating her abominably, and her children don't call her much. She keeps telling me I'm so lucky. I'm sorry for her but she makes me feel like I'm gloating, like I shouldn't have a good life when she is suffering so badly."

Natalie is a master at the Poor Me Posture. She plays the underdog who tries to build herself up by neutralizing the sibling who she feels is more successful and esteemed in the family. At the same time, she protects her self-esteem by reducing all of her sister's success to a matter of luck rather than hard work, a positive attitude, tenacity, courage, an ability to take advantage of opportunity, or anything else that is within one's control. She convinces herself it is not her fault—she was born under a bad star. And it works because Sarah feels she has somehow ended up with all the chips and must do her best to give some of them back to her sister.

•

Being hit with Poor Me is like fighting with your hands tied behind your back, because you are forced to defer to a person who
feels abused. You suffer from survivor's guilt, you're paralyzed,
feeling you have no right to succeed when your sibling hasn't
made it. At the same time, you hesitate to use your real assets because you have had the advantage of resources the other person
did not have. It differs from the previous techniques in that its
main objective is to make you sabotage your own position because
you don't want to look too good in comparison with your ill-
starred sibling.

Like the Guilting Gambit, it relies on guilt but has a different
slant. Guilting, rife with "shoulds," makes you feel bad for what
you should or shouldn't have done: "You should spend more time
with Mom." "You should have been here for me when I was so
sick." "You shouldn't have talked to her that way." Poor Me, on
the other hand, is designed to make you feel bad for something
you have in your possession, from material goods to good luck to
resources or attributes. Poor Me is much more subtle and difficult
to identify and combat.

•

Angela's sister Marjorie insists she is the ugly duckling in the
family and has never managed to find a successful niche for herself. "You were always so pretty, you always had plenty of men,"
Marjorie will say. Or "You're so lucky. Look at me. Everything I
do gets screwed up."

Angela, a talented actress, has discovered a surprising phenom-
enon through therapy—that she's been sabotaging her own career
so she won't be so clearly dominant over her sister. Always on the
verge of success on stage, twice in the past year she has found excuses to turn down excellent opportunities to play good parts because, without realizing it, she was afraid that Marjorie, who had
just lost another job, wouldn't be able to handle it. It's been that

way all her life. On the brink of success, something goes wrong in Marjorie's life and Angela falls apart.

•

So why does Angela fall prey to Poor Me? Not just because she feels sorry for Marjorie but also because it gives her something in return. Her rewards are that she feels flattered, significant, good, and successful in comparison with her sister. But while Marjorie is flattering her about her career or her men or her life style, she is undermining her as well by calling all of her accomplishments the result of good luck. So, at the same time that Angela's ego is pumped up, it is deflated. Believing Marjorie's premise that she got it all by accident, she becomes uncertain of her real abilities and self-destructs. That gives her a certain sense of worth because she has not totally outdistanced her hapless sister. If she doesn't succeed, she can console herself with the thought that she is a decent person.

And Marjorie, of course, continues to use this technique because she comes out looking like the good sport. Despite her difficult life, she can rise above her unhappiness and extol her sister's good fortune. She doesn't hold a grudge.

The Intimidation Offense

The Intimidation Offense, just the opposite of Poor Me, is used by one sibling to bully the other—and no doubt anyone else who presents a threat to his or her supremacy. Simple, unsophisticated, and highly effective, it is usually employed by the bigger, smarter, older, more favored sibling, who has the ability to frighten his brother or sister into submitting to his wishes. Often it's a power given to a child by the parent: "Mommy said I had to make sure you behave yourself. If you don't do what I say, I'm going to beat you up!"

•

One of our patients, Brian, has always been tyrannized by his next oldest brother, a gifted pianist. As they were growing up, the other children had to tiptoe around when Richard practiced, for fear of disturbing his concentration and precipitating a tantrum that invariably led to punishment by their mother. If Richard was annoyed with him for any reason, he would tattle to Mom that Brian was bothering him again. Although Richard became a high-school music teacher instead of a famed concert pianist, he still intimidates his brother by telling their mother everything Brian does that upsets him.

•

Other examples of sibling intimidation in our patients' lives include Mary, who remembers her sister hanging her from a tree limb by her ankles. Wriggling herself free, she never tattled because her sister told her that if she made trouble, she'd do something even worse to her.

And Melinda, who told a poignant story:

•

At 20, Melinda still fears her brother Danny, who discovered early in life that bullying somebody smaller not only worked but made him feel important and powerful. One day, when she was about 10 and Danny 13, her doting father gave her a silver dollar for coming home with good marks on her report card. Danny, who as usual did not receive praise or a silver dollar for his grades, wanted it.

"That evening, when Mom and Dad weren't around, he began knocking on my door in a steady beat—rap, rap, rap, rap. He didn't say a word but he wouldn't stop no matter what I said. He just kept rapping. I asked him, 'What do you want?' but he wouldn't answer.

"I knew he was insanely jealous because Daddy gave me that silver dollar. He had this look in his eye like he was going to kill me. Finally, after about half an hour, I gave up. I gave it to him. He took it and went into his room. That was it. I've never forgotten it and neither has he. I'm scared to death of him but I couldn't tell my parents. They'd just laugh at me. To this day, when he wants something from me, he starts rapping on a table or the wall and I just give it to him because I'm afraid not to, even though he's smiling like it's all a big joke."

•

Intimidation is a most effective tactic that works through sheer power, and it is responsible for many cases of sibling abuse, whether physical, sexual, or mental. It can be fended off only when the sibling on the receiving end becomes strong enough to stand up for himself or manages to place great distance between them. It allows the bullying sibling to gain a feeling of power in one area when he or she is feeling powerless in another. Melinda's brother Danny felt diminished and unloved when their father once again singled out his sister, the princess, as his favorite. By overpowering her in turn, he strengthened his ego, at least for the moment.

Being a tattletale is a less pernicious form of intimidation but it does the job. Brian's brother Richard, the pianist, used it adroitly. As a manipulative tool, tattling is a power play, a way to look good by making someone else look bad. Grownups who continue to practice this method don't consider themselves tattletales, but somehow they always manage to let other people know your failures and your shortcomings so they will look good compared to you.

The Paranoid Plotter

The person who uses this tactic against his siblings has perfected the ability to blame others, starting with his family, for his failures. The important feature of this technique is that the perpetrator tenaciously holds his ground, never wavers, never takes responsibility for a botched outcome, and always insistently lays the blame on someone else.

If you are the appointed villain, you will continue to be accused of misconduct even long after everyone else knows you aren't the culprit. The sibling who uses this technique believes that if she consistently blames somebody else, she will eventually rewrite history. This is the opposite of *Mea Culpa* and somewhat similar to intimidation by tattletale, but carried to new heights.

•

Certainly Harry was someone who pinned the blame on his brother Rob just about every time. Today, as he tries to sort out his feelings and understand his manipulative ways, he has begun to recognize that he has always used this behavior as a weapon, not only against his younger brother, but against his wife, his children, his subordinates at work, the waiters in restaurants, the clerks in stores. They are always to blame.

The oldest of five children, Harry was followed by Rob and then three sisters. While the girls fought it out among themselves, Harry and Rob took each other on as their siblings of significance. Rob, who resembled his mother's side of the family, was labeled the good boy, Mom's little darling, who received most of the hugs reserved for the boys. Harry was the image of his father, a large man with broad shoulders and burning blue eyes. Dad was a politician with cunning and ruthless ways, a man who could shake hands with you with one hand and bury a knife in your back with the other. Harry admired him enormously.

Obsessed by the need to be seen in favorable terms, Harry often used Rob's *Mea Culpa* stance to his own advantage. He recalls one day when he was 8 and Rob was 4. He had thrown the dog up in the air and it broke its leg when it landed on the banister. "My first thought was, where is Rob? I found him upstairs, lured him into playing on the landing, and tripped him so he fell on the dog. 'Look what you did?' I yelled, 'You hurt Rags!' Sure, it was a dirty trick to do that to him but I felt justified. If he was stupid enough to fall for it and would accept the blame, I was more than happy to give it to him. He was such a devious little wimp and Mom thought he was so wonderful."

Paranoid Plotters are logical and quick, always ready to pounce, and primed to remind their victims—and others within ear-shot—of their failings. After the dog incident, Harry rarely missed an opportunity to point out Rob's carelessness and irresponsibility. Harry was building a compelling case for labeling Rob. Once labeled, Harry could find lots more to blame on him, and Rob, in good *Mea Culpa* fashion, always managed to turn the blame to his own advantage.

The Insanity Defense

Frequently used by older siblings in an effort to prevent a younger brother or sister from surpassing them, the Insanity Defense is just what it sounds like—a threat of falling apart, going crazy, or at least becoming utterly unstrung and miserable. By convincing you that she is fragile and powerless, a person who can't take care of herself and is at the mercy of others, she becomes the sibling with the most power. This is a case of the meek inheriting the earth.

If you've come to expect a call from your sister in the middle of the night saying she thinks she's got cancer or she's considering the possibility of killing herself, you can be sure that she is responding to your successes, achievements, or pleasures. If, when you announce a positive happening in your life, your brother's customary response is to tell you that's great but his life is a disaster and he thinks he's going crazy, he is using his fragility to paralyze you. Of course, you don't want to be the cause of a breakdown.

This technique is often stoked by a parent who says things like "Your sister is so high-strung, you know how she gets. Try not to upset her. Don't tell her you got such a good mark on the test." You feel like a rotten person if you try to enjoy your own success.

•

Mary Jane called her sister one evening and told her she was getting married in six weeks. "I'm very pleased for you," Bobbi answered. "I'm really glad things are working out so well for you and I hope you'll be very happy. But," and she started to cry, "actually, Jim and I are having terrible problems and I can't see how I can possibly make it to your wedding unless you can postpone it for a while. In fact, I even tried to kill myself last week. I don't know what I'm going to do!"

•

Often subtle but always extremely controlling, this technique is designed to prevent you from surpassing or even competing with your sibling. It differs from the Sickly Syndrome because it almost exclusively involves psychiatric problems, usually depression. To be seriously depressed, perhaps even mentioning the possibility of suicide during desperate moments, is a surefire way to gain the upper hand over you, an unsuspecting brother or sister who is afraid of precipitating unhappiness. This method packs a big wallop when applied to the hand-to-hand combat of sibling rivalry.

Its powerful impact can be seen in the story of one of our patients who has been battling this technique for many years.

•

When Darcy calls her older sister Jenny and says, "How are you?," she hears, "How am I? Oh, you don't really want to know, do you?" The trap closes when Darcy insists, "Of course I do. I wouldn't ask if I didn't want to know. I'm your sister!" That's the signal for Jenny to unload all of her current problems.

Born into a rigid Greek Orthodox family that came to this country when she was 6, Jenny found herself angry and confused by Darcy's birth six months later. Jenny was shaken by the move, the language barrier, and the sudden appearance of Darcy. She was now expected to be a little mother to this baby who seemed to get all the family's love, while she felt relegated to servant girl. For her part, Darcy felt she was probably the straw that broke her sister's back. She remembers her mother telling the story of how Jenny's teacher pointed out that she was very jealous of the attention her little sister received. And she also remembers this sad tale, one of the first stories Jenny wrote in English:

"Once there was a princess, who the king did not like. The evil king gave her to a band of gypsies and later lied to the queen by saying the princess had run away with the king's enemy." The story went on to relate how the younger sister inherited all the money and all the love of the king and queen, married the good prince, and lived happily ever after.

This was the start of a pattern of sibling rivalry that lasted a lifetime. Darcy flourished and Jenny had an explanation for everything that didn't go her way. One day when she was 12, Jenny could stand no more of the darling Darcy and threatened her with a kitchen knife. That got everyone's attention and her father beat her for making such a bizarre threat. The beatings became a regular occurrence as Jenny continued to provoke her father in her desperate efforts to get attention.

"I always felt awful that Jenny thought I got all the attention and I felt guilty because I realized I really was the favorite, especially with my father," Darcy says now. "He never let her get away with a thing. I sympathize with her because our parents handled everything all wrong."

One day, soon after her eighteenth birthday, Jenny took an overdose of her father's sleeping pills. The father blamed himself because of his violence, the mother blamed herself for not intervening, and Darcy felt culpable because she had always been the favorite child.

Now Jenny became a burden to Darcy. The younger sister had to listen to her depressive thoughts and run to her aid when once again she threatened to kill herself. Jenny would say, "If you only knew what it's like to be so depressed that all you can think about is cutting your wrists. I have no life. I wish I were you." One weekend when her sister had made plans to go away to the beach with friends, Jenny tried suicide again, leaving a note for Darcy saying she would be better off without her.

"That did it," Darcy says, now married and the mother of three small children. "In all the years since then, I've never made a move without first thinking how it would affect Jenny. I do things but I always break the news to her very carefully, always reassuring her that she is wonderful, and always afraid of the consequences. I live with a sword hanging over my head."

The Shell-Game Scam

Siblings who use this method, usually an older sibling, are covertly competitive and constantly change the rules. It goes like this: They place a high value on a certain goal—marrying a handsome man, becoming a professional, being a good athlete, getting a degree, starting a business—for as long as they are winning in that arena and the goal seems to be within their grasp. But when they sense a sibling is gaining on them, they switch unannounced to a different goal, one they never seemed to value before.

If this tactic is consistently used on you, you will see that you are never allowed to be happy with what you've achieved. Suppose you get into law school or open your own real-estate brokerage, expecting applause. Your sibling, who once thought becoming a professional or starting up a business was the only road to happiness and freedom, no longer thinks it's so wonderful. Without warning, she's decided that artists are the only real contributors to society and she is now taking up sculpting.

•

Mary, for example, dated only tall, handsome boys who went out for football in high school, persuading her younger sister, Elizabeth, that looks were the most important feature to seek in a man. Elizabeth, thinking that she had won the competition hands down, eventually married a handsome man, a garage mechanic, rode around town on the back of a motorcycle, and spent her vacations fishing at the lake. Mary, however, not bothering to mention it, changed the rules. She ended up with a surprise candidate: a smart, short, homely, money-making doctor who preferred Jaguars and vacations in Italy. Elizabeth is wondering to this day why she has so little and her sister so much. She has been so focused on the competition that she hasn't stopped to find out what would make her happy.

The Enabling Technique

This is a common technique used by siblings to help a brother or sister indulge in a weakness—substance abuse, overeating, overspending, fears, promiscuity—while at the same time feel in control of themselves. Encouraged to continue the negative behavior, the recipient gets worse and in most cases eventually self-destructs. Because encouragement is accepted in our society as an act of kindness, the enabler tends to feel decent and good, a person who is trying to be helpful. What's more, he can sit innocently on the sidelines and bemoan the terrible fate of his brother or sister.

•

Sally used her skill at enabling to dominate her younger sister Robin who, she felt, took her place as the family princess when she was born. To Sally, Robin seemed to have all the attributes she wanted—good looks, intelligence, competency, the devotion of their parents.

Her resentment of this unbalanced picture surfaced in the only acceptable form of control she knew—encouraging Robin's narcissistic tendencies. It gave her an enormous feeling of power when she prodded her sister into having her waist-length hair cut short, an act that utterly dismayed their mother, and encouraged her to get the little bump removed from her nose, the first of a series of nose jobs.

"I don't understand why she is so focused on her looks rather than the important things in life," says Sally with an air of superiority. However, as her therapy progresses, Sally has begun to understand how, in her eagerness to prove herself better than her arch rival, she has exploited Robin's weaknesses.

•

Michael, too, played the enabling sibling who helped his brother to self-destruct.

It was Michael who introduced his younger brother, Jeff, to alcohol in high school when their parents were away one weekend. Later he introduced him to marijuana. When Jeff started doing cocaine and running out of money, Michael appeared to be an exceptionally good brother who urged him to get off the drugs but, at the same time, lent him the funds to live on. Although he never admitted it, even to himself, he knew that it would go to pay for his habits. Never, of course, did he tell their parents that Jeff had a problem.

It was Michael who bailed Jeff out of jail when he was picked up for drunk driving. It was Michael who covered for him after a binge. It was Michael who lied for him after Jeff was married, saying he'd spent the night at his house when he'd really been out doing drugs.

Until Jeff began treatment for substance abuse, he believed Michael was "the best brother any guy could have." But very quickly he began to see that his big brother had encouraged him to indulge in his self-destructive behavior. "At first, I thought I couldn't live without him, he was my savior. But then I noticed he was actually sabotaging my treatment, making plans to meet him in a bar, having something more fun to do when I was scheduled to go to an AA meeting. I finally realized that, if Michael had really wanted to help me, he would have told my parents and I would have been in treatment years ago instead of wasting so much of my life."

And Michael, after he had been in treatment for a while, was most surprised to find out that he had been ruining his brother's life with his good intentions. He never realized how he could be so subversive without even being aware of it.

The Denial Technique

If your brother or sister uses denial as a major tactic, you will have a hard time battling it because the perpetrators of this subterranean maneuver can rarely be made to understand that the way they view things does not necessarily match reality. Such people insist on denying what is obviously true because of their need to see things as they want to see them. The major purpose of the technique is to keep everything the way it is, to maintain the status quo. Denial is bliss and therefore extremely hard to combat.

•

Doris and Carrie are two sisters separated by three years. The older, Doris, was the family hero who did well in school and lived up to their father's high expectations with great flair. Says her sister Carrie, "I remember always feeling hopelessly inferior to my sister, who regaled my father with stories of her successes at school and in her ballet lessons. It usually happened at the Sunday dinner table. He'd sit there mesmerized, urging her to do even better. She was the star and I was the baby who went everywhere with Mom."

But in her envy, Carrie was denying the essential truth about her sister. Only in therapy was she able to recognize that those Sunday dinners were not wonderful for Doris. Doris pushed the food around her plate, eating only a few morsels, and then went to her room and did floor-thumping aerobic exercises for a couple of hours. Carrie attributed Doris's extreme thinness to her desire to be a ballerina and the excessive exercise to her insistence on staying in top shape for her performances. Even after Doris was admitted to a hospital for anorexia nervosa at the age of 17, Carrie went along with her father's opinion that it was just exhaustion.

Denial was Carrie's way of protecting herself from the tyrannical demands of her father, a perfectionist whom she knew she could never please. As long as Doris was his sole target, she was safe.

The Obsessive-Compulsive Technique

This is the most obvious maneuver a sibling can use to gain control over another. It works by frustration. When you try to control your sibling, he frustrates you by constantly obsessing about his never-ending concerns but never taking your advice, and constructing a complicated maze of ritualistic moves that are impossible to combat. The employers of this technique can easily become classic benevolent dictators, because once you accept their behavior as reasonable, you are locked into its control. Siblings who use it are remarkable for their tenacity. They cannot be made to do anything they do not want to do. They are masters of the power struggle and can match wits with anyone, simply by escalating their rituals to such proportions that nobody can possibly compete.

•

Alexis had been fussy about everything from the day her younger sister Tanya was born, while Tanya was perceived as the free spirit of the family who was entertained by her sister's perfectionistic rituals. The problem was that Tanya was not amused by them. Instead, they made her feel tormented and belittled and she was unable to defend herself against them. In treatment, Tanya said, "The joke was, until Alexis was out the door, everyone had to wait patiently because nothing would make her leave until she was ready."

Tanya remembers one night when she was going to her best friend's birthday party. "Mother said Alexis had to go with me because she didn't want to stay home with the babysitter who she insisted smelled of onions. Suddenly, Alexis was afraid of onions! She was afraid of everything. It was very unfair to have to take her to the party but Mother pleaded with me because she didn't want another of Alexis's panic attacks. So I took her.

"What a mistake that was. She must have ironed her dress ten times before it was right. Then we had to deal with her hair that had to be just so and required three washings. By the time she was ready, we were already an hour late. When I complained, Mother said I knew how Alexis was, just be patient. Finally we got there and there was a dog in front of the house that had to be caught and tied up before she would go in. She made a grand entrance and I followed behind, my dress all dirty from the dog, only to find my friend Janet angry at me for bringing my sister, forgetting her present, and coming so late.

"When I complained to Mother later, she told me that friends come and go but your sister is forever. Nobody ever said it in our family, but we all knew that Alexis was in total control."

Alexis is a classic compulsive who gets everyone's attention by involving them in her rituals. And as control becomes more important, such a person's behaviors become even more convoluted. Others come to expect them and quickly learn to alter their own desires to placate them. Tanya, for example, had already learned that not giving in to Alexis meant more torture. The ultimate weapon of compulsive people is their stubbornness, their control, their absolute refusal to do what they don't want to do. Although they are unaware of the motivation for their behavior, having been caught in their own maze, on some level they know they have won because you have been forced to cater to their demands.

The Narcissistic Knot

Narcissists erect almost impenetrable walls of self-involvement through which you, if you are unlucky enough to be a sibling who's getting the dubious benefit of their behavior, must pass in order to interact. For a while, they make you feel that you are consequential and important because you are in the presence of such a great person. But then when you walk away dazzled by their star quality and envious of their charm, you feel insignificant in comparison to them and disappointed by their lack of real concern for you.

Narcissists, in love with their own reflections, draw you to them while pushing you away because they cannot bear the burdens of intimacy and fear being held accountable in a relationship. Alternately your best friend and your most indifferent companion, they need you only when you help them shine.

•

Gerald grew up attuned to his sister Melissa's needs and devoted to her projects. She was an actress from birth, endlessly entertaining the family with songs, plays, and dramatic stories. As her younger brother and a bland person, Gerald gave her his full attention because he always felt he gained stature simply by association with such an exciting creature. "Melissa has a magical way of making me feel so important to her," he explains. "It wasn't until I realized that her entire focus was on herself that I finally felt disenchanted, disappointed, and used."

The week before he was to take his bar exam, Melissa broke up with her current suitor, one of a long string of boyfriends. "She insisted on calling me at all hours of the day and night, in tears, relating word for word over and over again every detail of their parting, while I pleaded with her to let me study. She got furious and yelled, 'How can you be so concerned about a dumb exam when I'm so miserable!' I flunked that exam. Like so many times before in my life, I had given up what was important to me—to cater to her—just so I could stay in her good graces."

The Hysterical Hustle

This maneuver is designed to turn the mundane into high drama, thereby capturing everyone's attention, bringing you into line, and relegating you, a less fascinating person, to the sidelines. The hustler has perfected the art of exaggeration, entertainment, and excitement, turning everything he or she does into an award-winning show. Superficial and transparent though this technique may be, it gives the brother or sister who uses it a surefire way to dominate the sibling competition. The person using this tactic usually feels he has very little to offer in the rivalry, so instead he flits from one attention-getting technique to another.

•

"In the blink of an eye, my sister can turn a nice calm ordinary situation into total chaos, escalating everything she does to enormous proportions. She had a cat. Lots of people have cats but her cat managed to take over the entire house," complains Zachary. "If she goes away for the weekend, for two weeks before and two weeks after, her suitcases and clothes are strewn all over the house. Everyone has to focus on what she's going to wear.

"I had a graduation party at the house when I got out of high school and somehow she forgot the date and invited a bunch of her friends over the same night so that my party got all mixed up with hers and wasn't really mine anymore. She fainted during my sixth-grade play when I was the star and that stopped the whole production.

"Somehow, wherever I went, my sister preceded me even though I was the oldest. She was known far and wide. 'Oh, you're Amy's brother!' She always stood out in a crowd because of the way she dressed and acted. She talked loud and her first car had a hole in the muffler so you could hear it two blocks away. Whatever she did, it was always very dramatic and it always overshadowed me."

The Splitting Setup

The Splitting Setup is a protective technique that is both sophisticated and powerful in the hands of an expert. The essential ingredient is an ability to "divide and conquer" any potentially threatening alliances by playing all sides against the middle. The practitioner of this gambit sets one sibling against another (or sometimes a sibling against a parent), and comes out looking good himself. If one of your brothers or sisters uses this technique on you, you can be sure he doesn't feel he's playing a leading role in the family drama and is trying to gain some significance in a very devious but effective way.

•

Suzanne was a real ace at splitting because she realized very early, as the only girl and youngest child of three, that she was going to have to split her two older brothers up or she would lose out. She had to wedge herself between these two forces because when they got together they formed an unbeatable team.

Her plans were simple: keep the boys at odds, each thinking the other was not to be trusted. When they were out, she would sneak into Chuck's room, take a favorite toy and put it in Johnny's room. Or she'd take Johnny's toy and put it in Chuck's room. Then she'd wait for the explosion when the boys came home. "You took my model plane!" "I did not!" "You're a liar!" "Call me that again and I'll punch you in the face!" The escalating battle would waft down the hall, bringing beautiful music to Little Miss Innocent's ears.

Choosing Our Own Defenses

You and your siblings have directly influenced the development of each other's defensive styles. If one of you took up the Guilting Gambit, for example, it is highly unlikely that you or another of your siblings also used it. Instead, like Joe, who responded with rejection, you have probably designed an interlocking tactic with damage control in mind. It's like a chess game. When one of you makes a move, the other responds with a countermove. When we are children the maneuvering is obvious, but as we grow up, our actions become more sophisticated and not as easy to spot. We develop a façade that hides our tactics as well as our motives.

Although all of us tend to make use of a few maneuvering styles as we encounter the daily challenges to our self-esteem, we each choose just one as our first line of defense. What is yours? And which one does your brother or sister usually use to keep the world, including you, at bay? It could be that your brother's preference is to apply intimidation when he senses invasion of his territory, while your sister lays on the guilt when she's feeling inadequate. Maybe your little sister plays The Baby who must be protected, while you tilt toward the Rejection Ruse when challenged.

All of you will continue to use these same maneuvers over and over again because you have learned them well and they usually seem to work. Even if they don't work most of the time, you feel safe with them and hope they eventually will. Although you may not consciously acknowledge your usual style of combat, in your heart you know what it is. You know your sibling's favorite defensive tactic too and *both* of you know exactly how far you can go with one another. That's one of the reasons siblings seldom break their connections even when the going gets tough. You *know* that your sister, hung up on intelligence, will become defensive at any suggestion of stupidity, and that your brother will put you down if you get bossy with him. There's no guesswork here—the whole routine is familiar and, in its way, very safe and comfortable.

Don't judge your own or your siblings' "standard operating procedure" solely in terms of their negative effects. Of course nobody enjoys being subjected to someone else's urge to prove his superiority over you, but remember that the techniques you all use were worked out long ago in your formative years. Back then, you were simply responding to your environment and trying desperately to protect your fragile developing egos. What's more, your choices were limited by the examples set for you, your own childish imaginations, the hazards of trial and error, and your level of maturity at the time.

As for your siblings, it's important to realize that they use their strategies not to hurt you but to protect themselves. Deflating your ego, relegating you to the inferior position, is only a byproduct of their efforts to feel important and in control when they are really feeling fragile *and* inadequate. So don't take it personally when you are on the receiving end of a hurtful maneuver but, instead, try to figure out why your brother or sister feels he or she is compelled to use it at that moment. The more destructively it is used, the more certain you can be that its proponent feels you are doing better than he is. Its purpose is not to make *you* feel small but to build *him* up. You simply got in the way!

If you feel permanently stuck with the tactics you have always used in dealing with your siblings, perhaps you can learn from our experience as therapists. One of the most important things we do in therapy is help our patients find new ways to deal with old problems and encourage them to try them out. When it comes to behavioral tactics, an area where change can definitely take place, switching over to new ways may be slow-going and difficult but it can certainly happen. This can give everyone an opportunity to break out of the old rigid mold and possibly find one that works better for all of you.

8

On the Job:
Siblings in the Workplace

Janie, 34, is the sister of a dominating brother six years her senior, who always led the way making the decisions, delegating responsibilities, and judging everything he saw. In charge of her much of the time throughout their childhood because both parents worked full-time in the family store, Harold made and imposed most of the household's rules and regulations. A kind and loving brother whom his sister adores but often resents too, Harold played the role of benign dictator.

In her job in a Wall Street financial firm, Janie has chosen an older man as her mentor. Although she is extremely intelligent and earns an excellent salary, she is his "right-hand man," a glorified secretary. She remains in that position despite her extraordinary abilities because it is terrifying to her to strike out on her own and take responsibility for herself. Her mentor, on the other hand, is an older sibling who is accustomed to having a younger sister take care of the detail work and look to him for leadership.

•

Everywhere you go—and the workplace is certainly no exception—you will find your siblings and the rest of your family. They will be disguised as other people, so you may not recognize them at first, but they'll be there and you'll treat them in the same old ways you learned back home, using the behaviors and defensive styles you perfected in childhood, whether or not they are appropriate in this new setting.

The truth is, you don't leave yourself behind when you go through the door of the office or the plant, nor are you rendered magically immune to the enormous influence your siblings—and, of course, your parents—have on the way you behave with other people. Often, the carryover of these childhood patterns leads to office conflicts or dilemmas that can place enormous roadblocks on your path to success. Nevertheless, you continue to use your own personal style because you are accustomed to it. It makes you feel safe and comfortable to reconstruct the world you know best, even when it produces sparks.

Re-creating the Family

Step into a new workplace and the first thing you'll do is re-create your family, unconsciously assigning familiar traits and roles to all of the players. Although the parallels may not exist in reality and the cast of characters may bear little actual resemblance to your relatives, you have the uncanny ability to see them as if they were the same people. You'll be unconsciously seeking the similarities—and you are going to find them. So, even when a brother or a sister isn't physically present, you may well encounter him or her at 9 a.m. every morning of your working life because re-creating your family on the job makes you feel right at home.

You will find that you involuntarily respond to one person just as you would to your younger sister who's a pussycat, to another as if he were your younger brother, the put-down artist, to a third as your showoff older brother, and a fourth as an amalgam of both your mother and your bossy sister. One of your superiors, who brings to mind your supportive dad, makes you feel warm and secure when he praises your work, while another, seen by you as similar to your manipulative older sister, elicits unsettling suspicions of dark ulterior motives when she does the same.

If, for example, you spent your childhood fighting with your younger sister for superiority, always watching your back, you're sure to run into your sister at work. She'll be there, disguised perhaps as the ambitious young fellow in the next office. Or maybe as the boss's secretary who, it seems to you, is waiting impatiently for the chance to move ahead of you. You will have made your new world over in your family's image, even though the players may not respond in the same way. Why? Because, after long years of practice, that is your orientation.

Remember that, like everyone else, you are susceptible to the effects of the self-fulfilling prophecy, which means that when you *believe* something will happen, you tend to act in such a way that you *make* it happen. If, for example, you believe that your boss doesn't like you—perhaps because you see him as the representation of your authoritarian father or your brother, your lifelong foe—you may behave in an angry or defensive manner toward him, which will make him mistrust you in return. The fact is, you determine your own reality.

Take a close look at your colleagues and you'll see how you have transformed them into your relatives and then acted as if they were the real thing. Usually you've cast the authority figures as the parents, and the co-workers or competitors as siblings, although there can be many variations depending on the specific circumstances.

Most important, try to figure out which person in this setting is the one who makes you feel the most wary and uncertain. If a colleague has the ability to "push your buttons" with ease, you can be pretty sure he or she reminds you of your SOS and so you unconsciously assign your feelings toward your real sibling of significance to this newcomer. Only when you recognize your transference of feelings can you begin to understand why you are having problems.

Playing Your Role

Perhaps because of your early experiences, your goal in life is to get by without too many hassles, or to be cared for by others, or to become the leader of the pack. You're destined to carry these same expectations with you to work and to anticipate the same results. If, for example, you were a younger sibling, the family mascot who never felt capable of successfully competing with your older brother, you may be a passive person, still seeking a leader. If, on the other hand, you were a rebellious younger sibling, then you're more likely to try to overturn the establishment and get things done in a new way. The forgotten child of the family? Then you're more likely to fade into the background, sit at your desk for years, passed over for promotion, expecting few rewards for your work and not at all surprised if you are the first to be laid off when times are bad.

On the other hand, if your style was to be the star, you will have to be the star in the office or you are not going to be a happy worker. Take Hal, for example.

•

Hal, five years younger than his sister but the oldest of three boys in his goal-oriented family, was the hero at home, the repository of great expectations and the accepted leader of his siblings. With high self-esteem, self-confidence, and presumption of innate power, Hal would stride into any room and take over as if he had announced, "I am in charge around here."

Starting as a copy editor for a trade magazine, he quickly rose to the position of associate editor, leaving his fellow workers— most of them glad, or at least willing, to be led—behind in the dust and was well on his way to the top. But here he encountered another star, a woman who filled the same function in *her* family and was not about to step aside for him. After a fierce competition for the job as editor-in-chief, she won. Hal stayed on as her deputy for six months, then quit when he was unable to accept his secondary role.

During those six months, he suffered from chest pains and constantly worried about his heart although his doctor assured him he was in good condition. He frequently woke up in the middle of the night in a cold sweat convinced he was being devoured by a lion. In therapy, he began each session with a discussion of his concerns about his health. Finally, after making a tenuous connection between his "heart pains" and his job situation, he recounted the time the whole family had gone to the amusement park. Although Hal, at 8, was desperately afraid of going on the rollercoaster, his older sister insisted, and after failing to talk his parents out of it by citing previous rollercoaster disasters, he went along because he was ashamed to admit his fear.

"I went but I was terrified. When Alice insisted on going again, I put my foot down and we didn't go, but I hated her for making me look like a wimp." Hal eventually connected that example of loss of power with the feelings he had when his control was eroded by his rival at work, realizing that control was his major goal and that without it he lost touch with his sense of self. His symptoms stopped but he was going to have to learn how to be more flexible and allow someone else—maybe even a woman—to be the leader once in a while.

•

If, instead of a leader, you were Goody Two-Shoes in your house, someone who never competed successfully with your older sister who constantly challenged the family rules, you'll be the one who never complains about overtime and who offers to go out and buy the birthday gift for the boss on your lunch hour on your own credit card. Meanwhile, there's another employee who's about to get the next promotion because she, like your sister, is a squeaky wheel who lets everyone know what a good job she's done.

•

Cynthia was the good girl in her family. She grew up in a household where her big brother's combative and confrontational behavior didn't pay off with their alcoholic mother, and she learned at an early age that being agreeable was the way to go. "I found out very quickly that fighting back got you nowhere except into very deep trouble. So I became the empathetic, cooperative one, the quiet child who could see everybody's side of things and tried to make everyone happy although whatever I did was never enough for my mother. I never fought back. Instead, I was the one who said, 'Sure, I'll do it.' It's amazing but my brother Gary, at the age of 42, still complains every chance he gets that I was spoiled and got away with everything. If I did, it was because I was cooperative and didn't make waves."

At work, Cynthia hasn't changed a bit. She is helpful to a fault. She has learned, however, that she would never get far in the corporate world because she could not delegate responsibility. "I'm not good at getting other people to produce," she says, "with my 'Please, if you think you can find the time, if it won't interfere with your coffee break.' I was always a good worker but my horizons were definitely limited. Now, however, as a freelance writer, my agreeableness is a positive. There are editors who love to work with me because I'll do rewrite after rewrite until they're perfectly happy."

Turning On the Charm

Family pets, the siblings who had the job of relieving family tensions with their humor and charm, aren't very different at work. They liven up the workplace because they're fun and they're good at coming up with creative ideas, but they tend to shrink from real responsibility.

Family pets have been known to develop fierce resentments toward their bosses, whom they unconsciously see as representations of their more aggressive, dominant, and usually older siblings or parents.

•

Martin, a talented engineer, never lived up to his potential because he persisted in tripping up his superiors. Adored by his peers and those on lower echelons because with them he was warm, funny, and attentive, he continually sabotaged his career by criticizing his superiors' judgments and questioning their decisions.

"My boss has always represented my big brother, no matter who he really was," Martin says, "and I couldn't wait to knock him on his ass. I had to take him on, show him I was superior." It was only when Martin finally understood, through therapy, that he had re-created his family in every job he ever had that he was able to behave in a way that better served his own ends. "I had to see that although my bosses were usually older and male, they were not my brother Burt. They didn't necessarily want to make a fool of me, they weren't out to embarrass me, they weren't trying to show me up. All they wanted from me was a day's work for a day's pay.

"You had to grow up in my family to understand why I had to prove they had no power over me. I was always on my guard with Burt, who was three years older than me. He felt it was his job to keep me under control by belittling me. I couldn't go after him directly, like really compete, I could only make sneak attacks. Humor was the best way, an acceptable defense in our house. If I could make everybody laugh, then I was free to blast Burt and get away with murder. Or else I'd pick away at him almost imperceptibly. I took those habits right onto the job with me and they didn't pay off."

•

Perhaps the experience of Barbara and her office colleagues tells the story of sibling influence in the workplace even better. The cast of characters includes Barbara, a top executive at a Fortune 500 company; her boss Andrew, an older male; a co-worker Jonathan and his pregnant wife; and Annabel, a pretty and charming young associate. All were to attend a company event and, to transport the group, two limousines were ordered, one by Barbara, the other by Annabel.

It was time to leave and only one limousine showed up at the curb. Barbara found herself compelled to know who had ordered it. Luckily, it was hers, making her feel more competent than Annabel. She then felt compelled to get into it, expecting Jonathan and his pregnant wife to ride with her so that the boss and Annabel could go together in the next car when it arrived. Looking back later, she realized that she had automatically assumed that the boss would want to travel with Annabel, the pretty young thing, instead of her. At this corporate level, however, the smart arrangement would have been to put the expectant couple and Annabel in one car, and Barbara and her boss in the other, or have the couple and boss go in the first car and her and Annabel go in the second when it showed up. In any case, she should have let her boss make the decision. And clearly to offer the first car to the boss, not to take it herself with Jonathan and his wife.

But now Jonathan, properly and corporately schooled, offered the boss his place in the car. The boss turned him down, not wanting to separate a very pregnant couple nor leave a very pregnant woman and her husband waiting on the curb. Annabel did nothing and allowed Barbara's mistake to really show. Finally, the second limousine came and the group set off—the boss skillfully maneuvered so that he and the couple were in one car, Barbara and Annabel in the other.

Why did Barbara expect the boss to want to travel with Annabel, the pretty young colleague? Barbara couldn't understand her own behavior or her own thinking process. When she was able to analyze her behavior, she realized that she saw Annabel as a representation of her younger sister, Alice. Alice had always been their father's favorite, a cute and perky little girl who had a way with men. Barbara saw herself, in comparison, to be a large and gawky woman with little charm. Feeling incapable of competing in looks, perkiness, or appeal to men, she focused instead on competency, responsibility, and getting the job done right. She automatically assumed the boss would prefer Annabel's company to hers, just as she felt her father preferred her sister's to hers. What she succeeded in doing was to make everyone uncomfortable and herself seem socially clumsy.

Fortunately, the qualities that gave Barbara strength as a child are still working for her. Her competency on the job is so superior that such errors in judgment are overlooked. But she is learning that many of the roadblocks she encounters on the path to success would disappear if she could leave her sister at home and go to work unencumbered.

The Same Old Defensive Techniques

You, like all of us, employ your own internalized patterns of behavior—the methods of psychological warfare you learned as a child—in the workplace just as you do everywhere else. You may use them in wholesome and constructive ways, or you may find instead that they seriously interfere with your ability to assess a situation you meet on the job.

It's when people are under particular stress that they are most likely to shed all pretenses and revert to the patterns of primitive defensive tactics that have always provided them with the greatest sense of protection, whether or not such tactics suit the situation. Feeling shaky, the Goody Two-Shoes becomes more obsequious, the Paranoid Plotter becomes more suspicious and secretive, the creative Rebel becomes more disruptive. The Poor Me becomes more pathetic and victimized, the Enabler more solicitous and destructively helpful, the *Mea Culpa* more passive-aggressive and annoying.

Some of the tactics they use will be effective in the workplace and some will not, depending on the circumstances. Suppose the most successful safeguarding method you learned in your childhood efforts to gain superiority over your sibling was to undermine her with the authorities, your parents. You'll undoubtedly find yourself using this technique at work. Somehow, you'll manage to tip the boss off to the fact that a co-worker isn't carrying his load and takes long lunch hours, whether it's true or not. We have all experienced the artful work of the office troublemaker.

•

Mindy, who worked in the secretarial pool of a large corporation, arrived one morning to be called into her supervisor's office and reprimanded for failing to finish her assignments that week. "Well," she replied indignantly, "Rita doesn't have as much work to do as I do. She should do it. Besides, haven't you noticed that she's always goofing off? I don't understand why you are criticizing me and not her." The baby of her family, Mindy had brought her doting family to the office with her. But unfortunately for her, they weren't really there.

•

If your style, instead, was to divide and conquer, you may find yourself setting up a conflict between two of your colleagues, leaving you in an advantageous position. Nicholas, the oldest of three brothers in an immigrant family, was the child who was counted on to guide their parents and help them assimilate in the complicated new world. It was a powerful role that he guarded zealously. When his two little brothers tried to compete, he kept them in their place by pitting them against each other for his favor, promising rewards to the one who sided with him.

In the workplace, Nicholas has continued to use that ploy time and again. Ever on the competitive alert, he has become the youngest managing director his bank has ever had. To combat his competitors, he inevitably selects the weakest of them and turns him into his right-hand man, favoring him with perks and privileges for his support, while at the same time setting him up to fight off his colleagues.

How Birth Order Affects Your Career

Your birth order is certainly not a completely reliable indicator of the career path you're likely to take, but it is one of the important factors that determines who you are and where you are going. Since many of your personality patterns evolved because of your placement in the family, giving you a view of the world from a particular vantage point, it can offer some explanation as to why, for example, most of the world's leaders were firstborn or only children, why middle children often do well in the corporate world, and why youngest siblings tend to become entrepreneurs or involved in worthy causes.

A look at your family's birth order can also help you understand the reasons for each of the siblings' choices of direction *within* their particular fields. On the basis of your personal traits and the role you have assumed in the family, both partly determined by your chronological place in the family, you will unconsciously navigate toward the area that best suits your special characteristics.

The typical firstborn sibling strives for a position of leadership—chief surgeon, manager, president, head waiter, litigator. The middle sibling may well be happiest immersed among other people in a midlevel position of responsibility within an organization—case worker, employee of a large corporation, family physician in a small town, secretary, company lawyer. The youngest, who generally strives to be independent and loves to turn things upside down, is more likely to become an entrepreneur, a researcher, a writer or artist, a worker for a cause.

Oldests at Work

Firstborns, similar in many ways to only children, usually gravitate toward jobs that require responsibility, reliability, loyalty, and hard work. Believers in their own supremacy, they don't mind starting at the bottom and working their way up because they have little doubt that their abilities will ultimately place them in positions of authority.

Accustomed to taking responsibility at home, oldests usually grow up to be people who are comfortable with leadership and go along with the establishment. They tend to be dependable and loyal, trusted by their bosses, and treated with respect by underlings who recognize their natural leadership qualities. Unlike only children, they have usually learned to be patient and tolerant with those on the lower rungs of the career ladder, but they are accustomed to being taken seriously. On the other hand, having been only children at least for a while, they identify with authority and are good decision-makers. Firstborns are often prudent, honorable, and law-abiding workers. Accustomed to power, they can also sacrifice their own needs and desires in return for control.

Onlies at Work

Only children, often forced to play the role of peacemakers for their parents and to resolve issues well beyond the scope of their years, develop traits that are useful in a work world that values the ability to negotiate and lead. Comfortable with authority figures, they get along well with those above them in the hierarchy, although they may seem overbearing to their peers.

Internalizing the extraordinary expectations of their parents, many onlies become driven, perfectionistic, hard-working, conscientious employees who will take on massive workloads without resentment. They are often not only eager but honored when they are asked to work long hours and accept enormous amounts of responsibility even when a raise or a title change is not the reward.

Accustomed to living in an environment where they have always felt on display, only children often take remarkably little notice of criticism. They simply don't hear it. On the other hand, their need to do things perfectly and to please their superiors makes them invaluable employees.

Middles at Work

For survival, typical middle children—especially the middles in same-sex and/or large families—have had to negotiate with both older and younger siblings, making them naturals at getting along with fellow workers. Less driven by emotion than oldests or youngests, they can be valuable employees because they have learned to be objective and cautious. In general, they are conscientious, careful, earnest, easygoing workers.

Middles tend to be quite modest about their successes at work because most of them have never had much attention paid to their achievements in childhood and rarely flaunt their superiority. Fearful of being seen as "different," they are seldom perceived as threats. On the other hand, they often resent not getting the credit they think they deserve and may long for recognition.

Not usually very self-revealing and tending to respect other people's privacy, middles do not burden the workplace with their personal problems, making them perfect team players. Although they are not likely to be good decision-makers and seldom feel capable of leading the troops into battle, middles are often excellent negotiators because they can see all sides of an argument.

Middles learn to fend for themselves at an early age, developing self-reliance, a trait that can be both a help and a hindrance at work. It is helpful because they are always willing to pitch in since no job is too difficult or beneath them. It is a hindrance, however, when they find themselves in positions of power, because, unable to delegate responsibility, they are apt to end up doing all the work themselves.

Youngests on the Job

Because not much is expected from youngest children as they grow up among their siblings, they tend to spend much of their lives trying to make a significant contribution to earn respect. Frequently, they don't decide on their careers until comparatively late in life because they don't know what it is they really want to do, and tend to be so insecure about their abilities on the job that they are especially sensitive to criticism. In combination with their natural rebelliousness, which makes them intensely dislike being told what to do, this inability to take criticism even when it is well meant often leads youngests to go their own way.

With their overwhelming desire to be independent and their tremendous competitiveness, they usually make better entrepreneurs than team players. They are often innovative and creative. They enjoy exploring new ways of doing things and may be pioneers in their fields. Not bound by tradition like their elder siblings, they search for the different perspective or approach. This, along with their creativity, highly developed listening skills, desire for the limelight, and ability to pick up on other people's feelings, allows many of them to find success in the arts.

In business, the same traits can lead to boom or bust. Saddled with built-in inferiority complexes as a result of their placement in the family, youngests have such little faith in themselves that they tend to resent and distrust people who help them, interpreting the help as an implication of their inadequacies. But they also resent and distrust those people who *don't* help them because that, to them, demonstrates a lack of caring and forces them to do something that deep in their hearts they believe they cannot do—take care of themselves. Youngests are always dependent for their self-esteem on the approval and acceptance of others, although this trait is often well disguised and may come out as bravado or cockiness.

In a corporate setup, youngest siblings are frequently the least cooperative employees, expert at undermining those in a position of authority and alienating everyone around them, but at the same time capable of using their charm and humor to bring a breath of fresh air into a stodgy firm.

Is This My Brother?

Treating a colleague as a representation of your brother or sister does not always work out to your best advantage because this person is obviously *not* your sibling. Maybe he shares some common traits, but he is somebody else and will not respond to you in exactly the same way your brother always did. Besides, he's been programmed by his *own* family. He will behave in his own tried-and-true pattern, the one he learned growing up at home with his own siblings and his own parents. And he too cannot easily change his ways, even when he wants to.

•

Patty found that out the hard way. The baby of her family, she was the cute little girl who could never quite get the hang of the copy machine and was incapable of finishing a project without constant reminders and assistance. She expected that everyone would take care of her just as her protective parents and two big brothers did. But the promotion she desperately wanted went to someone else.

"I was in a state of shock," she relates. "I thought it was a joke. My brother Jimmy always kidded me, telling me I couldn't have this or that and then, at the last minute, producing it. I guess I thought that's what was going to happen at work." But this was a place where being adorable wasn't anywhere near enough. Her employer needed somebody who could do the job, and that wasn't Patty.

•

Rose may have taken her boss, too, as a representation of her brother but she found out that what worked at home definitely did not work at the office. Rose grew up with a narcissistic younger brother who had no genuine interest in any of her problems or joys. While she was expected to be intensely concerned with his affairs, major and minor, hers held no importance for him. The only way she could get his attention was to make him feel bad when he overlooked her and then, when her frustration rose to an unbearable level, to overwhelm him with her anger. Only then did he hear her.

One day at work, she found herself uncontrollably screaming invectives at her boss without an inkling of where her intense anger was coming from. She had returned from sick leave only two weeks earlier, after a miscarriage and then corrective surgery. The boss, a man with other problems on his mind, said little about her ordeal and assumed an attitude of "Let's get on with it, we have work to do."

He wasted no time giving her several projects to accomplish within a short time frame, without consideration of her battered emotions or lack of physical stamina. The dam burst and what spewed out of her mouth astounded the both of them. Later she realized that her anger was really meant for her brother, whom she cued herself to see in her employer. Unfortunately, her tirade had different results because this man, after all, was not her brother and he did not feel guilty when she related her sad tale and definitely was not intimidated when she became angry. Instead, he responded in his own characteristic manner—with rejection rather than conciliation. She soon found herself looking for another job.

Your Siblings Help Determine Your Career

The influence of your siblings on your career choice may seem irrelevant, but it can play a very large part. Your birth order, along with your identifying labels, the defensive tactics you have perfected, and the role you play in the family are major determinants of the path you decide to take.

In most families, the parents decide on the general framework of the vocations that are desirable or acceptable for their children and encourage them implicitly or explicitly to move in that direction. From these parameters, the children of the family make their choices, usually picking areas that fit their individual traits, roles, and interests. If brothers or sisters have already taken over some of the possibilities, the options may then be fewer.

Although two or more children in a family may choose the same career path, it is much more likely that they won't. The exception is a sibling who is determined to surpass a brother or a sister, and therefore chooses the same field to endeavor to prove superiority. And of course natural assets and abilities may override one's best efforts.

•

Lisa, determined to be a model, went to modeling school, dieted and exercised, and endlessly studied the fashion magazines. She never succeeded in being accepted by an agency, however. Her sister Stacy, six years younger, on the other hand, was so startlingly beautiful that it required little effort on her part to become a top cover girl and earn her sister's virulent resentment. It took lengthy psychotherapy before Lisa overcame her envy and her sense of defeat and chose a more appropriate career for herself, this time as an aerobics instructor who eventually opened her own flourishing studio.

•

Usually, however, the oldest child in the family has first choice of careers and then fends off competition from the younger members. If the oldest child in a family that prizes professionals decides to become a lawyer because he is especially verbal and logical and has no head for science and mathematics, the younger siblings are not likely to compete with him in the field of law but may, with familial encouragement, choose medicine or education or engineering.

•

Earl came from a long line of physicians. His father, his grandfather, and his great-grandfather had been surgeons. So he, as the oldest male, never had a chance to consider another profession. His birthday gift at age one was a doctor's kit complete with stethoscope and blood-pressure gauge, and before long, his nick-name was "Doc." Don, only two years younger, got a teddy bear on his first birthday. The message from the family was loud and clear—Earl was to be a doctor and Don could be anything else.

Earl finished college, went on to medical school. Don, too, then expressed an interest in becoming a physician but when he announced that he was considering taking the medical aptitude tests, Earl, the concerned big brother, had a heart-to-heart talk with him. He explained that medicine was a tough field that required great dedication. Don, he said, seemed to be more interested in his social life than his studies. Earl also expressed his concerns to their father, and so his message was transmitted again—the day before the scheduled MCAT exam—when their father told him they would not have the money to put both boys through medical school. Since Earl was already two years into the program, he had first choice. Don understood the message and backed off.

•

Even if you do choose the same profession or vocation as your sibling, you are not likely to follow exactly the same route. Instead, you will tend to pick the area with which you feel most comfortable, the one that best matches your role in the family. While Earl, the older brother who was programmed to become a doctor, will undoubtedly be a surgeon like his predecessors because he is also a person who assumes leadership and takes risks, Don, if he defies the family and also goes into medicine, will be much more likely to choose another area, perhaps pediatrics or psychiatry, which will make use of his social skills and at the same time keep him out of direct competition with his big brother.

•

Antonio, 31, the middle child of three brothers, did choose to be an attorney, just like his older brother, Juan, but carefully stays far away from bankruptcy law, Juan's special field of expertise. Antonio had always felt drawn to the law, but because he sensed that option had been taken over by Juan, he took a job as an insurance broker. Encouraged through therapy to "follow his bliss," however, he finally went to law school at the age of 29. But he flatly refuses to take any cases involving bankruptcy because he does not want to compete head to head with his brother. Juan, for his part, has always claimed he's delighted Antonio is also a lawyer, but the moment he feels threatened is the moment he goes into the infantilization stance that he used so effectively on his younger brother when they were kids. "All of a sudden," reports Antonio, "he's treating me like I'm an idiot, hovering over me, checking my work, going into long diatribes on basic aspects of the law. It makes me angry and it makes me unsure of myself, too. In other words, it works!"

Siblings Play a Part in Success or Failure

Perhaps it seems preposterous that your siblings as well as your parents have the power not only to determine when you're allowed to be successful and when you're not, but also just *how* successful you are allowed to become. But this too, although it may not be readily apparent, is an area in which your family can have a profound influence because they can discourage you from prospering in your chosen career. They also have the power to manipulate the timetable of your success or failure by encouraging you or draining you of the motivation you need to move ahead.

•

June is a talented 26-year-old actress who seems to have spent most of her adult life deliberately avoiding success. Although her sister Shari, 29, was her mother's favorite, June was the favorite of no one. She was conceived in an attempt by her mother to hold on to her faithless husband, but the maneuver failed. Before she was one year old, her father left the family and she promptly became an inconsequential member of the household. As June grew up, she understood that to her mother she was the symbol of a failed marriage, to her father she was a child-support check, and to her sister she was a resented contender for their mother's attention.

As a result, she received little positive attention until she had grown up and began to achieve some success. An actress who had trained very hard for years, she was chosen for the cast of a Broadway musical. Her mother was excited at last, thinking she would now bask in the glory of her daughter, the famous stage star.

Shari, who had gone from job to job without settling on a career, wasted little time however in developing a severe case of panic anxiety. From early childhood, when she developed respiratory problems, she had been a hypochondriac. Her main symptom now, in addition to gasping, sweating, and palpitations, was agoraphobia, fear of going outside of the house. She was unable to work and was afraid to be left alone.

Of course, the attention that had briefly focused on June was immediately shifted right back to Shari. Neither June's mother nor Shari could make it to opening night of the show, her mother began to resent the nights she had to stay home while June was out "having fun," and most of June's earnings went to help pay for her sister's psychiatric treatment. Finally, under great stress and fearing even more rejection by her mother, June managed to get herself laid off from the show. Now Shari made an amazing recovery. Before long, she went back to school while June wondered if she could ever be a successful actress again.

When June came into therapy, what seemed perfectly clear was that Shari had not been able to tolerate her younger sister's threat of greater success and the possible shift of maternal favoritism to her, so she had unconsciously resorted to illness as a way of defeating her sister and returning to her childhood status quo as the featured daughter. June, in the meantime, picked up on all the hints and carefully avoided surpassing Shari. Although it took her many months to come to accept that her family may have had anything to do with her career, she has developed considerable insight into her plight.

•

The story of Allen and his younger brother Pete provides an-other illustration of the influence of siblings on success in the workplace. Allen, six years older than his brother, had pretty much raised Pete. Their alcoholic mother and ineffectual father were emotionally and physically unavailable much of the time, but Al-len had always been there to act as Pete's surrogate parent. He did the shopping, prepared the meals, made sure Pete did his homework, and earned Pete's devotion.

Allen got a job with a large corporation, and when his brother finished school, he found a job there for him. Both of them did extremely well as systems engineers. But one day Pete, who was blessed with considerable charm and humor, was offered a job as a sales manager for the company, giving him an opportunity to make much more money and move up the ladder. He attacked the work vigorously, using his charm to great advantage, and soon Allen was getting word from all quarters that his brother was doing a fine job.

But it wasn't long before Pete found himself becoming nervous and depressed and finally he was asked by his boss to get psycho-logical help. In therapy, he revealed that he felt he owed his life and his job to his big brother. Unable to bear the guilt of surpass-ing him, even though Allen said his success only reflected well on him, Pete sabotaged himself instead. At the same time, he hated feeling indebted to his brother. In one session he said, "I realize he was the key to my survival in that dysfunctional family and I love him, but I feel angry because he always seemed so superior and self-sacrificing. It's awful that the one person who loved me is the one I'm hurting to get ahead."

•

What happened to both June and Pete was that they uncon-sciously understood that they were about to surpass their older siblings, who had been given first crack at success. As a result, they unraveled. They regulated their own abilities, held themselves back, in an effort to keep things in the proper familial order.

Such psychological dynamics reside in the remote territories of our unconscious and are usually firmly resisted in therapy because understanding them requires a reevaluation of our relationship with parents and siblings. Although experienced therapists may recognize the pattern very quickly, it is often a long and painstaking process for patients to examine all the pieces, accept them, and then defy the family law. What usually motivates them to change is a realization that the rewards of liberating such core feelings can be enormous. These rewards are usually most immediate and most obvious in the workplace, and patients soon recognize that they can make dramatic, positive changes in their relationships on the job by sorting out their sibling dynamics.

There are two likely reasons why such rapid changes are possible in the context of work. First, there may be no need for a direct sibling confrontation because much of the effort goes on inside your head and involves people who have much less investment in your behavior than your real brothers or sisters. Second, in our culture, people are readily convinced that they have an unalienable right to be successful if they work hard. They understand that a sibling or a parent who stands in the way of that success is doing them an injustice, and once they feel entitled to do well, it usually follows that they will.

June and Pete represent so many of our patients who have come to understand that their career aspirations have brought them into conflict with the status quo of their families, and although they understand that their attempt to change will be met with resistance, their courage has been fueled by their strong desire to succeed.

Sibling Dynamics in the Family Business

In the United States, many businesses are family-owned but few of them manage to survive into the third generation. While a family business can strengthen the relationships among the members, it is much more likely to tear them apart. The reason, in most cases, is that the business is treated as an extension of the family, with members taking their roles and rivalries with them into the intensely competitive business environment. As a result, most siblings find it almost impossible to cooperate with one another in the ways that are necessary to run a successful company. Sibling rivalry, never completely shed and especially susceptible to reactivation when money and power are involved, becomes the catalyst for disaster.

The roles assigned in childhood to each of the siblings, so functional for family survival, are usually extended to the business setting where they may not be functional at all. Often the oldest son—or occasionally the oldest daughter—is given the leadership role because he has been the assigned leader among the children. He may not be the best suited for the position and may not even want it, but he's got it, while others in the family may resent the assignment and at the same time are afraid to try to push past him.

Also, siblings who are not interested in the business and would do much better in other fields are often held captive by family ties. Everything becomes more complicated when aunts, uncles, cousins, second cousins, and especially in-laws become part of the mix.

Working among facsimiles of your siblings is not the same as working with the real thing. In a family business, you have your actual brothers and sisters to deal with, people with whom you have always battled for control and supremacy. Objectivity is often the least of your concerns when old rivalries take over and cloud your judgment. You will continue to carry around in your head the model you grew up with, perhaps the intimidated younger sibling who has always been dominated by a big brother, or maybe the big brother who continues to look over his shoulder in fear of being overtaken by a more aggressive, rebellious sibling.

In most cases, the family business survives without splitting the family apart only when the assigned roles are valid or readjusted according to reality, when expectations are not beyond what each person can deliver, when "loyalty" is suspended so that judgments or performance and the monetary compensation can be fairly evaluated, when the family members share their feelings with each other, or—as is the most usual outcome—when outside directors are hired to bring in fresh insights and mediate differences.

Coming to Terms

When you understand that you are the same person on the job as you are everywhere else, a person with hangups acquired in childhood and never completely left behind, you can see that it pays to look closely at your sibling relationships. Although you may easily detect the influence of your parents on your adult behavior, you may have never seen the connection with your brothers or sisters. Nevertheless, you have taken them—as well as your parents—to work with you. It's human nature. When you accept that fact, you are in a better position to recognize familiar attitudes and self-protective mechanisms, to quit confusing your colleagues with your rivalrous siblings, and, where appropriate, to make efforts to modify behavior that isn't working out to your advantage in this new setting.

Obviously, the shop is not the only place where we are sure to use the behavioral patterns developed at home. Sometimes even more obvious is the effect of families on our love lives, to be explored in the next chapter.

Romance: Your Siblings and Your Love Life

A face across a crowded room. A laugh, a look, a tone of voice, a few words of conversation. You may have met only a couple of moments ago but it feels like you've known each other all of your lives. Your eyes shine, your heart pounds, your fingers tremble. You're in love!

Is fate, accident, or coincidence responsible for our crushes, our lovers, our selection of mates? Far from it. Everything we do in life is an act of choice, although we may take advantage of opportunities that come our way. In most cases, we select our romantic partners, temporarily or permanently, because we "recognize" them, feel a mysterious connection to them. Somehow—for better or for worse—we know them, sensing a mutual understanding that makes us feel comfortable using our accustomed ways of navigating in a confusing world. What's more, we are attracted to this same kind of person over and over again.

What are our chances of success? Is the relationship with our newfound love destined to be healthy, happy, and enduring, or filled with discord and conflict—or somewhere in between? Have we chosen a mate who fills our needs, fits comfortably into our learned patterns of behavior, provides the support we crave? One way to help predict the future is to examine our choices, noting how they relate to the patterns we know and the experiences we have had growing up with siblings and parents.

Most of us have little awareness of the powerful influence our brothers and sisters may have on our love lives. The tendency to duplicate in the present the relationships we've had in the past with our parents has been endlessly discussed in the psychoanalytical literature, and we all accept the possibility of choosing a partner who resembles our mother or father. But picking a partner who is similar to a sibling is just as likely, even though we may not want to acknowledge that our little sister or big brother has the power to influence such an important part of our lives.

The behavioral patterns of our families are often echoed too. If we grew up with a philandering parent, for example, we are much more likely to wander ourselves, while if fidelity was valued at home, we will probably pride ourselves on being faithful. This is true even when we are determined *not* to repeat the patterns of the past. In our practice, we are always hearing patients say, "I don't want the kind of marriage my parents had." Nor, frequently, do they want a replay of their relationship with a sibling. But history has an amazing way of repeating itself.

When you consider the differences between parental and sibling love, you will see that, ideally, parents offer us unconditional love, love with no boundaries or limitations. Siblings, on the other hand, place conditions on theirs: They threaten to walk away from us, to withdraw their love, and we believe them. The menace of a brother telling us, "If you don't walk the dog, I'll hate you forever," or a sister demanding, "Give me your doll this very minute or I won't invite you to my birthday party," imprints us with our first fear of the withdrawal of love. We will experience this kind of conditional love, love we are always in danger of losing, in every relationship we may ever have, except, of course, with our own children, where the miracle of unconditional love is reborn.

"Marrying" Your Sibling

Siblings as metaphors are often so subtle that they are hard to spot. You don't readily see your older sister in your husband or think of your younger brother every time you look at your wife. But they are often there, just as they are on the job, represented by the same behavioral styles that you know so well. As in every other area of your life, you are trying to make yourself feel at home, using your same old pattern of presentation with lovers and spouses, whether or not it fits.

•

Robert, a tall, handsome man of 42, falls in love over and over again with highly competitive, ambitious women, fights them to the death, and, when he has won, leaves them in the dirt. He knows this kind of woman intimately because she is a duplicate of his older sister Tracy, his sibling of significance, whose rivalry with him has ended in estrangement. "This certainly is not what I really want," he insists in therapy, "and I don't understand why I keep choosing that kind of woman." But when he meets up with softer, more introspective, less challenging women, "the chemistry" isn't there and he quickly finds a reason to end the affair.

•

The truth is, you are just as likely to "marry" a sister or a brother as you are to "marry" one of your parents, choosing a partner who resembles a sibling or perhaps the qualities of a couple of siblings or a combination of a sibling and a parent, in your efforts to recreate the well-established emotional themes of your life. In fact, your romantic partner is inevitably a pseudo-sibling, with whom you will see the clearest reflections of your childhood relationships.

Taking Along Unresolved Conflicts

If you are still in major competition with your siblings, still feeling the reverberations of unresolved rivalry, you are more than likely to extend those same competitive feelings into your romantic relationships, where they may well lead to disaster. You are in for potential difficulties if you connect with a person who is a stand-in for your sister with whom you have never stopped battling or your brother who overwhelmed you with his superiority (or whom you defeated with yours). Carrying those unresolved conflicts into a new relationship can doom it to failure if you don't recognize the familiar dynamics and make some efforts to modify your behavior. The big question is, how do you alter the pattern? First, you must become aware of what you are doing and that's consistently picking the wrong person. Second, start looking around for someone who is not a reincarnation of the sibling you've always tangled with or is at least a much less extreme version. Stop choosing the one who has always automatically turned you on and force yourself to give a different kind of person a chance to prove himself. Get to know him well. Meanwhile take note of the tactical maneuvers you typically use and try to use different ones. Better yet, do all of the above!

•

Althea was consistently drawn to "cool" men, men with style, calculating men who used her and finally rejected her. If you asked her to define "cool," you would get a bewildered look and "You know, cool!" It turned out that "cool" was her older brother, a man who had always impressed her with his ready answers, his proper attire, his self-assurance, and his dominating personality. He was someone she greatly admired but could never be.

As a child, she was so eager for his companionship and acceptance that she stole money from Daddy's pockets and Mommy's purse to buy him candy and trinkets. She worked at after-school jobs and loaned him the money so he could take his current girlfriend to the movies or buy a new shirt. She did his bidding and ran his errands so she could be rewarded by his approval. The darling of his chauvinistic father and devoted mother, Ben used her as he did everyone else in his life and occasionally, in their teen years, magnanimously included her in some of his plans.

When it came to falling in love, Althea always chose a glib, cool, slick, narcissistic man very much like Ben. She did his bidding adoringly, showering him with attention, gifts, and invitations. Although the results were inevitably disastrous, it wasn't until she was in therapy that she began to understand her attraction to this kind of man and to start appreciating men who had the ability to give back to other people.

•

In a romantic relationship, you will, of course, use the same repertoire of behavioral tactics that you learned at home. If you have become proficient at guilting your brother, you will undoubtedly do the same with your mate if it works. If you are a Paranoid Plotter, you will find somebody to blame—maybe a person who is a gifted *Mea Culpa*. If an intimidator, you'll look for someone who can be overpowered. Once you identify the familiar dynamics when you are dealing with someone who is *not* your sibling, try to figure out their origins in your childhood sibling rivalry and then share your insights with your mate. Your relationship will have a much better chance to grow when you both understand the roots of each other's behavior. You will be more tolerant of each other's automatic defenses and better able to help each other modify those behaviors that can damage or destroy the relationship.

Although the re-creation of your family is played out to some degree in all marriages, it is important to recognize whether you are perpetuating a constructive or a destructive, and therefore hazardous, pattern of behavior.

•

Kate is an example of someone whose relationship worked out to her advantage. She grew up with a protective and powerful older sister who paved the way for her throughout their childhood.

A shy, introverted little girl, Kate depended upon Danielle to fight her fights, ward off the criticisms of their harried mother, and attract her playmates. Danielle, though often irritated by this small and constant appendage, nevertheless provided shelter and continues to this day to remain the role model for her sister.

Kate, very pretty and obviously seeking protection, attracted many suitors. The person she finally chose was a counterpart of Danielle, a man who shields her from the buffeting blows of the world and, although often impatient with her timidity, satisfies her greatest need. "The minute I met Gerard," she says, "I felt secure. I knew he was the one for me. We fell in love on our first date." Gerard satisfied his own needs too by marrying Kate. A man who had never felt important, always overshadowed by his two younger but smarter brothers, he hunkered down with Kate and they both found home.

•

For Stefan, however, replaying the sibling roles did not result in a healthy outcome. Stefan always felt sane and competent, far superior to his sister Ellie. Growing up in a chaotic environment, with a submissive mother and a verbally abusive, alcoholic father, Stefan survived by playing the role of the family hero whose successes made up for much of the household's misery. Meanwhile, Ellie was the appointed "lunatic," the scapegoat on whom everyone else dumped.

Although he constantly denigrated his sister and always felt superior to her, whom did he choose to marry? A woman just like Ellie, a victim, a person with an enormous feeling of inferiority and a tendency to fall apart under stress. Stefan's wife helps him maintain his feeling of sanity and competence by allowing him to stand on her shoulders with his head above the water, just as he did with Ellie. He feels free to be the superior being and knows exactly how to deal with her periodic fits of tears and complaints of great injustice. He puts her down and she accepts it, feeling she must be to blame for the treatment she receives.

Fortunately or unfortunately, with therapy Stefan is becoming too healthy for this marriage to last, unless his wife can manage to stop being so helpless and needy.

•

The duplication of a sibling or a parent in a romantic partner, of course, is never exact and it is the contrasts between family and lover that often make the difference between success or failure of a relationship.

•

"I guess you could say I married my sister or at least the healthier aspects of her," relates Andy, who as a social worker has learned to recognize the patterns within. "My sister Betsy is nine years older than I am and so is my wife. They are both strong capable women. But Anna, my wife, is the youngest in her family, just as I am. So she understands me and my rebelliousness as my sister never did and I fit beautifully into her need to be organized, reassured, and in control. We both were looking for recognition of our value. The moment I met her, I knew we belonged together. I needed an army in a marriage, a person with great strength, a partner who would help me fight the battles of life, and that's what I got. Anna was not only very much like my sister but she was also very much like me. She was obviously a winner. I learn from her, admire her tremendously, and have tried to follow her example."

Other Influences Too

Siblings not only determine what you find attractive and whom you choose as a partner, but they influence your romantic life in several other, perhaps more obscure, ways. They can, for example, act as barometers that forecast things to come and as signposts to values that were not overtly transmitted by your parents. They may use their influence to stabilize the family power structure. They may select their mates before you do and so make you feel your options are limited. They can set the pace of events for you, orchestrating your wedding date, when or if you have children, buy a house, get a divorce, remarry, retire. They can appear as metaphorical representations that come to life in your interactions with your spouse. They may rival or denigrate your mate or come between you and a prospective or actual partner, betraying your confidences, exposing your secrets, even driving suitors away. They can compete with you for the bragging rights of the next generation—the virtues and accomplishments of your children.

Siblings as Signposts

The way your brothers or sisters live their lives may well turn out to be your pattern, too. You can't help but wonder, for example, when something goes wrong in a sibling's marriage, whether it is going to happen in yours. Perhaps, you think, you have both chosen unwisely or acted foolishly because of the examples set in your common upbringing.

•

Nina watched and learned from her older sister, Ada. After thirty years of marriage and two grown sons, Ada found a note her husband had written to his secretary and carelessly left on his night table. It told her he planned to leave his wife for his new lover. Ada, devastated, called her sister to share her anguish. Nina was left to wonder whether such behavior had precedent but couldn't find a frame of reference. Nevertheless, she began to be suspicious of her own previously unquestioned spouse. He was to be watched closely because Nina had learned, via Ada, that formerly trusted choices could not be relied upon.

It all became clear when their father had a stroke and rambled on about a woman with whom he had had an affair for many years. Had their father's example subtly affected Ada's selection of a spouse? Or Nina's? It may sound farfetched, but children know when there's trouble in the family; they can sense when there are secrets not being revealed. For Nina, the warning was clear: Be vigilant or her father's ghost could haunt her marriage as well. If Ada had chosen a man who replicated their father, maybe she had too, and she also had to be careful not to let her and her sister's suspicions drive her husband into the arms of another.

Stay Just the Way You Are

An additional pressure on your love life may be exerted by siblings who count on you to continue playing the role you have always assumed within the family. If you are the designated scapegoat, for example, you may continue to be blamed for the collective problems, or, as the caretaker, pressed to continue the job of tending to the family's well-being despite your new responsibilities.

•

Laura, 34, is the oldest child in a family that included one boy a year younger than she, and three much younger sisters. Teamed up with her brother as her chief ally and competitor, Laura played out her role as the caretaker/manager of the siblings. "I was the sensible, serious, responsible one. No fun at all," she relates. "I followed the rules and made sure the others did too, which they resented, of course." Her brother, she relates, was "an airhead," off in his own world, easygoing, funny, extravagant, and adored. "My role was to keep him—and the rest of them—out of trouble, while his was to get everyone to lighten up."

Today Laura still plays the same role, married to a man who grew up with two overachieving older sisters and who continues to play his part as family pet—lovable, humorous, and irrepressibly optimistic. There's friction when Laura becomes too overbearing, and when he refuses to make decisions, but they are both comfortable doing what they do best. Meanwhile, she remains in charge of keeping her four siblings in touch and rushing to their aid when they ask for her help, a frequent event, because it is still expected of her whether or not it interferes with her own family's life.

The Status Game

Siblings can affect your romances in more ways than serving as models for your mate or objects of your accustomed behavior. Competing siblings may make your respective suitor/spouse the prize in the game of one-upsmanship: Who has selected the more agreeable, respected, understanding, affluent, and wonderful partner? Who got the mate the other sibling would have liked to have had? Who's the winner?

Between serious competitors, finding a superior mate often becomes a major goal. You—or your sibling—may pick a partner who is rich, respected, beautiful, because the connection with this person confers a feeling of importance and a status higher than your sibling's. This form of competition can be the most alienating aspect of unresolved rivalry because, when brothers or sisters continue to compete through the accomplishments of their spouses or children, the game's scope is greatly expanded, exponentially increasing the opportunities for family feuds.

Sometimes a brother or sister, still suffering from residual competitiveness, becomes a rival to your mate, criticizing your choice in an effort to feel superior to you. He may even try to drive away prospective or actual partners by betraying your confidences or making sure they are apprised of your weaknesses.

Mates are often used as spokespersons, too, the ones who do the dirty work in the fight against a brother or sister with whom a sibling fears to tangle directly. Like a ventriloquist's dummy who speaks the lines for his master, the spouse takes over the fight in the service of the partner.

•

Randall, married to Suzy, is known in the family as a tyrant who doesn't allow Suzy to breathe without checking with him first. He assumes the role of king who demands and gets her total attention, overseeing her activities and doling out a small household allowance every week, which she must account for in full detail. Meanwhile, Suzy, who has no time for her own pursuits, feels guilty about leaving the entire care of her chronically ill father to her sister Georgina, who is outspoken in her resentment about it.

Why does Suzy put up with Randall? Because, among many other reasons, she is using him as a tool to gain the upper hand over Georgina, her SOS, who she felt spent her childhood victimizing her much as Randall does. Without Randall, Suzy has no excuse for not freeing Georgina from all of the work and responsibility of their father. By blaming everything on him ("Isn't he awful? He won't let me!"), she turns the focus on him and away from her and feels, at the same time, that she is evening the score with her sister.

•

In many marriages, a mate is sent directly into the front lines to do battle with a sibling. As a personal pit bull, the partner takes the initiative and the heat. This was the case with Alicia and her sister's husband. "My brother-in-law Bob was my sister's mouthpiece," says Alicia, "something I didn't understand for many years. I think she felt she could never win because I was always much tougher, the one who always had to have the last word even though she was older than me. But she needed to get at me somehow and I finally realized she was egging *him* on to do battle with me. Every time we were together, Bob would go after me, criticizing, blaming, arguing. We agreed on nothing. We'd get in terrible battles because I fought right back while my sister defended each of us to the other and came out looking like the good guy. It wasn't until they were divorced that I began to realize what had been going on. Now she had to fight for herself, and she *still* used him! She did it by saying, 'Bob always said you'd do anything to get what you want,' or 'Bob tried to tell me how self-centered you are and he was right.' Finally, one night we had it out. I told her to speak for herself. She did—and I did—and ever since then we've been more honest with one another and getting along a lot better."

Often mates play another very subtle but effective part in the sibling battle. When a new spouse is brought into the family, the usual response of the siblings of the same sex to this newcomer is to compare him (or her) to themselves. When she (or he) is similar to them, it is seen as a compliment, especially if the marrying sibling is held in great esteem by the family. But when she is dramatically different, it is usually taken as a put-down or even an insult, and certainly a rejection of what they represent. And they are usually right because their sibling may well be attempting to come out ahead in the lifelong power struggle by using another form of the rejection game.

•

Take the case of Marguerite, the princess of her family, who brought home a prospective husband who was the opposite of her two brothers. Her fiancé was tall, blond, muscular, and affluent, while her brothers were rather small, plain, hard-working, poorly paid, and intellectual. This charming intruder made them feel inadequate and unattractive, and terribly slighted by their sister.

Siblings and Timing

Your rivalry with a sibling can help decide when you meet and marry your mate—or even when you get a divorce. Marriage is one of life's landmarks and frequently the sibling who accomplishes it first is considered the winner of the race. In days past, it was understood that younger siblings had to wait for those in line ahead of them to marry. Today, of course, this is not so, but all the same we remain conscious of when it is "our turn" and when it is not and frequently feel persistent internal pressure to perform—or to not perform. And frequently, we make decisions based not on our real feelings, but on sibling rivalry. The pressure to keep up, especially with an SOS, can be healthy when it spurs us to action that's right for us. But it can cause serious problems when the primary incentive, whether we realize it consciously or not, is to surpass our siblings.

•

"Marriage was far from my mind when I took the train to New York after college graduation," Helena told her therapy group. "I was going down to celebrate my kid sister's engagement to Will, whom she'd met in the eighth grade. Arlene always does everything by the book, nothing spontaneous. I was the impulsive one, doing whatever felt right at the moment. And I was always the first, the frontrunner, of the two of us, but now she was getting ahead of me. As far as I knew, that didn't bother me a bit. I had big plans that didn't include a husband just then.

"I was sitting on that train reading a romance novel when a voice from over my shoulder said, 'You're not going to read that junk, are you?' I turned around and there was this great-looking guy smiling at me. We hit it off immediately. Matt was going to New York to look for a job. Well, it was love at first sight. I took him to the engagement party and showed him off, and four weeks later he proposed. The next week, we got married, a month before Arlene's wedding. Matt got a job as a salesman and I went to work as an editorial assistant at a magazine. Truth to tell, I married a stranger but it worked out well enough."

Six years later, Helena's marriage seemed shaky. "Somehow I find him annoying these days," she said. "Even the way he sneezes is irritating." With questioning, the therapy group soon discovered some of the truth. Arlene, the kid sister, who had divorced Will six months earlier, had now met a handsome young man named Peter, a lawyer in a prestigious firm, scion of a prominent family, and had announced her plans to marry him. Suddenly Matt didn't look as good to Helena as he once did. Now he suffered by comparison to Arlene's prospective husband. Once again, Helena's life was being run not by her real choices, but by competition with her lifelong rival, her sister.

•

It is not even very unusual that, when one SOS gets a divorce, the other one does too. This copycat behavior is all in the service of maintaining the sibling status quo, as Dan found out. Dan and David were brothers, both of them married with two children, successful careers, houses in the suburbs. They had been fairly close as children but had drifted apart through the years, making appearances together only at major family functions.

When Dave's twenty-two-year marriage broke up, however, he began calling Dan at least once a week. "That was O.K.," says Dan, who was our patient. "I understood he was out there all alone and I wanted to help him. And to tell the truth, it felt good that my big brother was coming to me for support. But then I started feeling uneasy. Every time I turned around, Dave was asking me to go on a trip with him, hunting, fishing, snorkeling in the islands. I went once or twice but I really couldn't afford it, and besides, I felt guilty leaving my wife and kids to go on a singles vacation.

"It finally dawned on me that Dave would have been really happy if my marriage broke up too. Misery loves company and he didn't want me to be happily married when he wasn't. I'm sure he didn't admit it to himself, but he wanted to feel better off than me. When I realized what was going on, I backed off and I think he understood why."

Birth Order: Can It Affect Your Marriage?

An awareness of how firsts, middles, and youngests tend to behave in the context of romantic alliances can provide a few useful clues about how your potential partner views the world.

We know that oldest children in a family tend to be conscientious, law-abiding, trustworthy, self-assured, straightforward, and diligent. With all those attributes, it would seem that they would make wonderful mates.

However, they share common tendencies that may affect their love lives. For example, firstborns are notorious for being bossy. Most of them love to be in charge and in control. This can be especially troublesome when an oldest sibling chooses another oldest because they both want to be the leader. Two extremely powerful firsts will do nothing but clash until it becomes clear who will dominate—or the affair blows apart. Bossy firsts usually do better with more compliant partners, usually middles or youngests, who may better tolerate or even enjoy their take-charge attitude.

As perfectionists, the result of bearing the major responsibility for their parents' expectations, typical firstborns are frequently demanding and critical. They expect too much from themselves as well as others and find it hard to allow other people's mistakes to pass without comment. This intolerance applies not only to their mates but to their children, who are often subject to higher standards than they can possibly meet.

Firsts are born competitors and they can make a competition out of anything, from who earns the most money to who does the dishes faster. Usually not the most romantic of lovers because they tend to lack spontaneity, firstborns' lovemaking tends to be a ritual for them and, like everything else, can be turned into work. In fact, work often dominates their lives, relegating everything else to second or third place.

Middle children, on the other hand, are likely to be masters of compromise. And to flee from difficulties, doing anything to avoid a fight. Easygoing, friendly, tactful, unassertive, typical middles find that their major problem as mates is their inability to make decisions. "Whatever you want to do," they say, placing a large burden on their partners, although they are also usually willing to do much of the dog work that follows.

The charm of their tendency to shun the spotlight and not to take credit depends on the strength of their mates' desire to want these positions for themselves. Married to controlling firstborns or attention-hungry youngests, middles may represent perfection if, in return, they are given encouragement, reassurance, and loyalty. Married to other middles, however, they may not set off enough sparks to maintain mutual interest. The best advice for those who marry middle children is to be aware of their fears and to encourage them to stand up for themselves and take pride in their accomplishments.

As parents, middle children tend to be understanding and loving but easily manipulated. Discipline and consistency don't come easily to them.

People who grew up as the youngest members of their families also share common tendencies that can affect the way they relate to the loves in their lives. In general, youngests are socially adept, adventurous, creative, rebellious, fun-loving, attention-craving. At the same time, they tend to suffer from low self-esteem and the fear of being left out.

Because they are accustomed to having other people take responsibility, youngests shun major decision-making and expect others to take care of things for them—but resent them when they do. Often very competitive, they regard themselves as instant experts but may not recognize the importance of hard work and long hours. Impulsive, they are typically unconcerned with the consequences of what they do today, expecting everything to work out tomorrow without much effort on their part. This means they may be big spenders who fail to plan for the future, a trait that seldom leads to marital bliss.

Marrying a youngest usually requires that you must dispense strong doses of patience, reassurance, and nurturing, and, in return, you get the benefit of creative ideas, optimism, and enthusiasm. Your relationship will be more successful, too, if you remember that concealed beneath that patina of self-confidence, youngests almost always suffer from feelings of inferiority, inadequacy, and dependency, and therefore match up best with supportive partners who shore up their faltering egos.

Putting Your Insights to Good Use

Recognizing that your sibling relationships may have a profound effect on your love life won't take the magic out of romance. Instead, it should enhance your feelings and help prevent unhappy mistakes. You can still fall in love, you can still stay in love, you can still have that feeling of exhilaration and of walking on air, but perhaps you will have a better understanding of why you feel the way you do. Gaining some understanding of why a certain person sends chills up and down your spine can help to minimize the feelings of loss, rejection, betrayal, and pain when a romantic relationship goes sour—and it can maximize your delight when it goes right.

•

Take the case of Norma, for example. She had come into therapy after an unhappy marriage that lasted six years and a most unpleasant divorce that dragged on for three more. She claimed she had married a man who reminded her of her exciting, supportive, and uncritical mother, and then he had turned on her mid-marriage when he became demanding, unsupportive, and judgmental. Everything that went wrong seemed to be her fault.

After putting much effort into examining this marriage, she saw that she hadn't "married" her mother at all. Instead it was her brother, whose habit had been to praise and cajole her into feeling safe, only to pull the rug out later. Always resentful because she was Mom's obvious favorite, Jerry spent his childhood trying to prove her bad in Mom's eyes by manipulating the situation so he was never at fault and she was always to blame. On the "plus" side, Jerry was amusing and dynamic, the one who made a dreary house and a spartan life style fun. He had a way of taking the ordinary and making it seem exciting. All of Jerry's qualities were to be found in Norma's ex-husband, but somehow she had never recognized the similarities.

During two and a half years of therapy, Norma dated at least twenty-five men, first finding herself strongly attracted to men like Jerry and her husband. "But I became more and more aware of what I was doing," she says, "and I began to understand how I was perpetuating a pattern that could only end in unhappiness for me. Before long, I was passing up dates with men I once would have loved to go out with and getting interested in guys I would have called dull before. It's amazing how a little bit of self-knowledge can save a lot of heartache."

10

As Time Goes By: The Phases of Sibling Relationships

Alex and his sister Gladys, 80 and 75, hadn't seen one another in thirty-two years, each stubbornly clinging to major resentments toward the other. But now they sat eating dinner together like two old gray elephants sharing the same watering hole. For years, Alex had hoped that the phone would ring and it would be Gladys calling to find out how he was or to apologize for what she had done to him. And Gladys had spent a lot of time praying that he would "see the light and accept God's will." But neither had made a move to meet until now.

Gladys, born beautiful, was from the start the star of the family. Pampered by her adoring parents, she grew up to become a well-known dancer in the style of Isadora Duncan. "She was the talk of the town, always on the society pages, dating this famous athlete or that rich man. And she was our big hope, the one who would take this lower-middle-class family into high society. She finally married a wealthy businessman from an uppercrust family," is the way her brother tells it. "I, on the other hand, was pretty ordinary, bright enough but kind of dull and steady. I became successful in banking, married and had a family, all professionals now, but I felt my accomplishments were always considered of little consequence compared to hers.

"I never understood how I'd had a five-year head start on her and yet she surpassed me like I was the kid brother. It was like I was standing still and she was running flat out. When we were young, she was doted upon while I felt like I was just tolerated. I worked very hard for everything I got." Alex became the family caretaker. He was responsible, reliable, and dutiful. "All my life I tried to do the right thing," he says, "even when it was hard."

Nevertheless, the siblings got along well enough because he too bought into the family myth, basking in his sister's reflected glory and catering to her wishes.

The feud between the two ignited after Gladys, following a bitter divorce that left her impoverished and forced to take her children to live with her widowed mother, converted to Christian Science and soon won her elderly mother over to her religion. By this time, Gladys was too old and overweight to return to modeling. Alex, working hard at his career, kept in touch, making sure all was well.

The fights began when Alex realized their mother was very ill and insisted she see a doctor. Gladys refused to allow this because of her faith. Finally, the courts supported Alex in his demand for medical attention, but it was too late and their mother soon died. Gladys assigned him the blame because of his lack of faith, while he blamed her for her absolute trust in hers. That was when he discovered that his mother's entire estate had been willed to his sister. "It wasn't much but it mattered. I knew my sister had talked her into giving it all to her," he says. From that moment on, he and Gladys never spoke again.

So why, after all those years, did they decide to meet now? Says Alex, "I felt it was time to make peace. Obviously, we're both going to be meeting our maker any time now and we should try to forgive and forget. Maybe it sounds stupid but I feel, even if she did her best to ruin my life, she is my sister, she's family. She's the only one left."

He wrote to her, then called several times, and finally the meeting took place at his son's house with all the family, her children and his, in attendance. Despite the passage of years and all that had happened in the meantime, the two promptly took up their old roles. Gladys, still eager for center stage, told funny stories and tall tales while Alex found himself once more playing second fiddle to the star. "But it was worth it," he says, "because somehow I feel much more comfortable now with that connection repaired. No more major unfinished business."

•

During a lifetime, the intensity of the relationship between siblings waxes and wanes, going through periods of closeness and times of quiescence or even estrangement. In an almost predictable pattern, most people are extremely close to their brothers and sisters in their early years, pull apart as adults, then feel an irresistible urge to get back together again as they grow older.

Here is how we see the major phases of a lifetime and their effects on how brothers and sisters tend to relate to one another through the years.

Childhood

The developmental phase of childhood, from birth to adolescence, is a formative time of tremendous tension because the family is amorphous, always changing, reshaping, and rearranging itself as new children are molded into their roles and given their own identities. Eventually, the family dynamics crystallize, hardening this new little unit into a unique shape that is likely never to change substantially again.

In childhood, brothers and sisters are by necessity a major part of one another's lives, often spending far more time together than they do with their parents. It is the beginning of relationships that will endure for a lifetime, in most cases longer than any other they will ever have. Living together, eating together, playing together, fighting together, defending themselves against authority together, facing the same family problems together, produce a relationship that is both intensely intimate and openly competitive.

Brothers and sisters will probably never again be as close physically or emotionally, nor will such tremendous turmoil and unpredictability embroil them ever again, making the rivalry between them in these early years keen, open, sometimes even brutal and violent, with brothers and sisters serving as one another's direct objects of rage and envy. At the same time, strong alliances, love, and dependencies may also be forming and reforming among them, serving to create even more tension within the group.

•

Christine remembers one afternoon when she was 10. Her mother had gone to the store, leaving her and her 12-year-old sister, Ellen, alone in the house. "We got in an awful fight, I don't even remember what about, and we beat each other up. I remember hitting her with a wooden hanger and scratching her face and she bit my arm and pulled my hair. By the time Mom got home, the place was a wreck and both of us were in tears."

That same evening, Christy went into their room and found Ellen crying on her bed because a classmate she thought was her best friend at school had not invited her to her birthday party. "I put my arms around her and tried to comfort her because I couldn't bear knowing somebody was hurting her. She seemed so fragile and vulnerable and all I wanted to do was protect her. Isn't that odd, considering that, just a few hours earlier, I would have cheerfully killed her if I could? It didn't make sense."

•

Parents are obviously the greatest force, often almost to the virtual exclusion of any other influence, that affects the relationships among their young offspring. Parents, whose love and approval, attention and time are the prizes for which their children actively compete against one another, are the source of all power. So this is a time when healthy and sensible parents make great efforts not to play favorites or give any of their children crippling labels, a time when they step in to define the boundaries, the rules and regulations of sibling warfare, so that everyone is treated as fairly and as predictably as possible. Obviously, this is not an easy job since there's no child who doesn't constantly test just how far he can go, both with parents and siblings.

As a child in a young family, you continually jockey for position among your siblings, making monumental efforts to gain superiority over them and trying to get just as much as you possibly can of the love and attention available from your parents. If your brother or sister seems to get more than you do, you feel they must have some magic you don't possess or that they have stolen the prize that was rightfully yours. You want to take it away, to hurt them for getting it. Reality doesn't matter. What counts is your perception of the inequality.

Becoming Yourself

This is when you become the kind of person you will always be. That is not to say that, in later life, you can't learn new behaviors through circumstance, friends, mentors, marriage, careers, therapy, parenthood, all of which have an impact on your personality. But it is at home, with Mom and Dad and brothers and sisters, that the real core of your being is formed.

Now is when you acquire your labels, those special traits that are assigned to you, defining you and making you unique. At the same time, you are developing the role you are to play in the family and perfecting your own individual style of interacting with other people. In fierce competition with your brothers and sisters, you carve out your own territory and learn how to erect powerful defenses against invasion by the others. By the time you are six or eight years old, you have developed the basic coping style that you will use for the rest of your days.

It's the time of life when you discover the most effective methods of affecting the behavior of other family members in your efforts to get the power you must have for your psychological survival. You find out that threatening your brother with exposure of his sins is an excellent way to force him to knuckle under or lay off, that whining at your mother will lead her to give you what you want, and that rejecting your sister almost always gives you the upper hand, at least for the moment.

Even putting on a pretty face, perhaps acting like "the little mother" or the paternalistic big brother, doesn't mean that sibling rivalry isn't hard at work. Instead, it can be a deft disguise, an adroit way of gaining power and superiority over a brother or sister.

•

Melissa at 8 is the middle child, sandwiched between two boys. Although her older brother, the family star, is out of her reach and pays little attention to her, she has assumed total control over the youngest, who is 5. She has taken him on with the goal of making sure he doesn't become more powerful than she. One day, when little Harry asked the nanny if he could go to a sleep-over at his friend's house, Melissa noted the nanny's uncertainty and immediately took charge. "No," she said, "you can't do it because Mommy wouldn't like it. You stay home and we'll play games." And that was that, no sleep-over. Undoubtedly, throughout their lives Melissa will continue to play surrogate mother and caretaker while Harry will try to wiggle out of her control using his own tactics of rebellion or ridicule.

•

This rivalry, like its other forms, is natural, developmental, and acceptable. This is the way it's supposed to be. This is how people learn, how they grow, and how they become who they are.

Important Differences

As we have discussed, coming into a family as the first child is very different from arriving second, third, or even further down the line. And the condition of the marriage when you arrive changes the way you are greeted. Major tensions between the parents as the children are growing up are often acted out among the siblings, creating resentments that can last a lifetime and color the nature of the relationships forever.

•

Margot attributes much of the rivalry she still feels toward her sister to the struggle for supremacy between their parents. Margot and her older sister, Lee, were assigned labels right from the start, labels that became so ingrained that they have never been lost, even though each sister has always wanted what the other one got. "She was smart and I was fun," Margot says. "She always wanted to be fun and I wanted to be smart. She defended her role by telling me how dumb I was and I kept her out of my domain by incessantly playing the clown and letting her know I thought she was boring.

"I spent a lot of time examining our relationship when I was in analysis, and what I saw was that we were used as pawns in our parents' conflicts. I'm sure they had no idea what they were doing but I think Lee took on the part of the smart one with the radical opinions because my father, who was uneducated but extremely intellectual with radical opinions, needed an ally, and my mother, the more social one, chose me to be on her side to balance things out."

•

In this phase, sibling relationships are affected by the family dynamics in yet another important way. Children can't risk taking aggressions and hostilities out on their parents—or other adults—for fear of potentially disastrous repercussions. So they tend to aim their anger and frustration at much safer, more available and vulnerable objects of wrath—their siblings—often causing over-whelming problems for siblings who are not directly to blame. In more families than most people care to believe, sibling abuse—physical, psychological, sexual—is common during these early years.

Adolescence and Young Adulthood

As children start to become adults, they turn outward, separating and distancing themselves from the family. Now the head-to-head rivalry between siblings typically diminishes as youngsters move from the close, intense relationships within the family to relation-ships with outsiders. Although they continue to measure themselves against one another, they are now graduating to competition with the symbolic image of a sibling rather than the actual person.

Because they carry their attitudes and techniques with them when they go out into the world, they run into the very same dif-ficulties and successes they had back home. A girl who is accus-tomed to being the leader at home, for example, will make herself the leader in her new social world or end up mighty miserable. A young person who feels inferior to his brother will take that feel-ing into his high-school classes and unconsciously find a smart "brother" there who makes him feel inferior once more. The ten-dency to repeat and duplicate patterns of behavior is powerful.

However, some reevaluation is possible, too. The same young man may discover he isn't as incompetent as he thought, achieve some measure of success now that he is in another setting, and re-vise his view of himself.

At the same time that brothers and sisters pull away from one another in this phase of their lives, they often feel the pangs of loss or even rejection as the world intrudes upon that close sibling relationship. The intimacy they experienced as children, two kids struggling together against the same strong forces, has to dissipate as each starts dating, goes off to college, moves out of the house, gets married, leaves town. So they may attach themselves to people who remind them of their retreating siblings and try to fill in the gaps their loss has made in their lives.

•

"When my brother Spencer went to high school, I felt abandoned. He made a lot of new friends there and he didn't want to spend time with his kid brother anymore," says Mike. "Now he was more interested in girls and hanging out. I even missed the fights we used to have. He wanted no part of me and I was devastated.

"By the time I got to high school four years later, he was off to college and out of my life for good. Yes, I had his room and his collection of model planes, but it wasn't like having *him*. At around the same time, even my best friend Butch began to annoy me. He was a nice guy but too blah. He used to help me plot and plan and battle my brother, but, with my brother gone, we had no one to plot against. Then I met Ed who was a lot like Spencer— tall and thin, argumentative, selfish, confident, sure. Just like Spencer, he thought he was somebody special and deserved all the good things in life. It was a very comfortable relationship, it felt natural, like we'd been friends forever. So he became a substitute brother, somebody for me to challenge and look up to at the same time. We've been friends for over twenty years now."

•

As young people move through adolescence and early adulthood, the power the family holds over them diminishes. Siblings gradually give up their struggles with one another over strictly family-defined, metaphorical, egocentric rewards, and start competing for more tangible and measurable society-defined accomplishments. In other words, now you compete not so much for Mommy's attention or one more piece of cake than your brother got, but rather for superiority in school or on the football field, for more friends than your sister has, or more success in the workplace. These are the goods that everyone else wants too.

At the same time, you are testing out your identity on a new playing field, wondering whether what the family dynamics have assigned you in labels and roles is truly who you are. Using your siblings, especially your sibling of significance, as your yardstick, you make judgments about your accomplishments in relation to the rest of the world. If you feel you are measuring up well and that your image of yourself is consistent with the way you have felt within your family, then you will probably navigate through adolescence and early adulthood fairly smoothly. But if the world as you saw it in childhood doesn't correspond to the world you now encounter, your rivalry with your siblings whom you see as surpassing you will probably continue unabated right into adulthood.

•

Jason was five years younger than his brother James, so when he arrived in high school, James had already gone off to college on a football scholarship. Jason recalls, "I remember the biology teacher telling me that he hoped I'd be more of a student than my brother, who he described as a jock and a ladies' man. It was that day that I realized I had a chance to be my own man at last. The teacher's words stayed with me and I made up my mind to be different from my brother. I worked really hard and that teacher sure was surprised when I was valedictorian of my class and won my own scholarship—to a good college. In our family, I'd been brought up to believe I was the brain and James was supposed to be the athlete. Well, it all worked out."

Starting New Lives

As young adults, siblings usually distance themselves from one another as they form new alliances and embark on lives that may be almost completely independent of their brothers or sisters. This is the time to make moves that may take them many miles from home geographically and emotionally, when new priorities take precedence and already existing animosities become reasons to preserve the distance.

One of the most critical events in a life history of a sibling relationship takes place when one of the siblings gets married. Although, on the surface, a marriage is usually viewed as a welcome and positive experience for everyone concerned, most siblings of the happy bride or groom cannot escape experiencing ambivalent feelings.

The marriage of a sibling represents a loss of innocence that can never be regained. Most other rituals in life do not so dramatically alter the allegiances that have been formed over so many years. A brother or sister often meets this intrusion with great resistance, interpreting the event as being left behind both literally and symbolically.

•

"When my brother got married, I felt surprisingly sad and rejected," says Dick. "Although we were furious competitors and hated each other much of the time, it was a real loss, almost like losing your first love. Everything was different for a lot of reasons. First, he no longer lived in the same house with me, not even for those brief college vacations. Then, I had to stop looking at him like my big bully brother and start seeing him as a grownup person with responsibilities, who was preoccupied with his own life and not me anymore.

"I remember feeling that his wife would now have all his attention and I would be relegated to the status of second-class citizen. He married when he was 23; I was 18 and in my second year of college. The emotional shock was much more than I would have anticipated. It changed all the dynamics of our relationship because he now had a formidable ally in his wife, who had brains, money, and social acceptability, and I was unimportant. He promptly bought a house, had kids, and was a grownup. I was only five years younger but I was still a kid. Suddenly we were worlds apart. Add to that the fact that all I heard from my parents was 'Jim this' and 'Jim that.' I decided it was all his wife's fault."

The Middle Years, 25 to 45

In the middle years, a period of maximum opportunity and capacity, the tendency is to distance yourself even more from your siblings as other priorities take over your life. Now your interests and activities are likely to focus almost exclusively on people and places outside your original family's perimeters. As you settle down in the context of your new world, you have more important matters to attend to—the pursuit of an education, the establishment of your own home, the demands of a spouse, a new family, a burgeoning career, job changes, disappointments, triumphs, troubled teenage children, social acceptance, money problems— and your siblings and your parents cannot command your full attention. Your primary allegiance is to a different world populated by a new cast of characters.

A few of us, especially if we feel major resentments toward a brother or a sister, lose contact altogether at this time (although complete alienation is rare), while others remain tightly connected and always in communication. But most of us simply drift apart, a little or a lot. We're busy leading our own lives. We don't forget our siblings and we don't abandon our family loyalties, but their importance loses much of its original intensity as more immediate concerns overwhelm the system. Our consciousness of our siblings and our relationship with them is nowhere near as significant to us as having a good marriage and a successful career.

This doesn't mean, however, that we don't remain in major competition with them. Just because you haven't seen your brother or sister in twenty years or don't think about them from one week to the next doesn't mean the rivalry has magically evaporated. It may go underground, where you think it is firmly secured beneath a mound of civility or geographical distance, but it takes only a crisis or an important change in any of your lives to trigger it off again. A marriage, a divorce, the birth of a first child, a promotion, a move, the illness or death of a parent, an inheritance dispute, can disrupt the familiar patterns of behavior and reactivate the same old feelings of "You were always Mommy's favorite" or "You always got your own way."

It is almost as if drifting apart makes the potential for explosions more likely. You've been busy minding your own business when suddenly you are faced with competition from your brother or sister. You are caught off guard and all the old rivalry pops right out uninvited.

•

Fran was three years older than her brother Bruce. She was planning her 20-year-old daughter Allison's wedding, an affair that had the potential of putting an end to all chances of reconciliation between her and her brother. The last time the two families had been together was seven years earlier when they had spent a weekend at the beach. It was a disaster because Allison and Bruce's son Jeff, a year younger, had been found naked in bed together. Fran blamed Jeff and Bruce felt she was overreacting to a couple of kids experimenting with one another. After that, the two siblings spoke only occasionally on the telephone and saw each other rarely, especially since Fran lived on the East Coast and Bruce in California.

Allison, who came to us for counseling, remembered the look on her mother's face when they discussed the possibility of inviting Uncle Bruce and his family to the wedding. "She said it was up to me and I said it was O.K. if they all came. Actually, I thought they'd add a little glamour because Uncle Bruce was now a well-known film director. But my mother launched into a tirade about how cousin Jeff had tried to rape me when I was 13 and how she didn't want to be reminded about that by his presence at the wedding.

"We finally decided to invite only Uncle Bruce and his wife and not my cousin. That wasn't good enough for my uncle, who said he'd be happy to come but only if Jeff was invited too. My mother and he had a blowup on the phone that was beyond comprehension. Needless to say, Uncle Bruce did not come and they haven't talked to each other since.

"I secretly think Mom set the whole thing up because she'd always felt Bruce was the fair-haired boy who got all the attention when they were kids and I think she thought he was going to upstage her at my wedding. I certainly was not going to tell her that I was the one who invited my cousin into my bed that night seven years ago!"

Competition Forever

Even when you distance yourself from your siblings, you never stop measuring yourself against them, especially your sibling of significance, and trying to prove to yourself that you occupy a superior, or at least comparable, position. Although the playing field has changed, you still conduct ongoing reassessments of your accomplishments and assets, rating them against your siblings. Almost anything can become a competitive component as you tally up who's got the better life, the better job, the superior spouse, the most impressive house, the smartest children, the most achievements.

But you don't compete only with your real siblings, but also with what you have internalized about them. As we have already discussed, you'll replace the originals with reasonable facsimiles, people in whom you *see* your brother or sister.

The Late Middle Years, 45 to 65

When the major milestones in our lives have passed, most of us experience a rebirth of intimacy with our brothers and sisters, especially if we had a close relationship earlier on. You might even say we're mellowing. Now we start yearning to dispose of the emotional baggage left over from our childhoods and feel a need to draw closer to our roots. Now security, peace, and familiarity usually become more important. So we make moves to rebuild our foundations, reduce the emotional distance between us, make friends again, be part of each other's lives once more, get involved in the destinies of one another's families. We look for opportunities to explore early experiences with those who were there with us.

By the time brothers and sisters have passed midlife, many of the issues that built barriers often don't seem quite so important anymore. You're not so preoccupied by outside problems as you used to be. The rivalries you once felt are still there but they've usually become muted—now it doesn't seem so important that your sister has made more money in business or if her husband has more prestige than yours. You may even have replaced your envy for her accomplishments with respect and admiration. Meanwhile, she's more willing to forgive the superior performances of your children and the fact that you spent your childhood pushing her around. The field becomes more level as the inequalities gradually lose their potency and you begin to view your siblings as people who give you comfort because they share the same memories and face the same concerns about the future.

At the very least, things have become quite predictable by the time you've hit 50 or so. Neither you nor your siblings are likely to make major changes that will upset the balance between you— you're probably not going to have a new baby, get married, become an astronaut, go to medical school, take over the company. You're either on the road to becoming president or making a fortune, or you're not. You know which one of you was Mother's favorite child and you've accepted it. This is the time of life when you are likely to continue being the person your siblings know, and they are likely to remain familiar and predictable to you too. All of which makes it much easier to say, "That's how they are and they're not going to change" and come to terms with them. You think about them more, feel closer to them, and become more approving and accepting of them. In addition, you are more likely to use them as confidants and advisers than you did before.

After all, many of your friends have come and gone, maybe even your spouse and your parents have done the same, the children have flown the nest and perhaps established their own families, and who else is there to care about you? Just as important, who is going to be there if worse comes to worst? The answer in most cases is your siblings, who share your roots and who you often feel freer to turn to than your children. Now's the time to heal old wounds and make peace, if it hasn't happened yet, because of strong mutual needs for a sense of family.

Problems with Parents

This phase of life, however, is often driven by the aging of your parents. Getting through parental illness, disabilities, death, and estates is an enormous challenge to sibling relationships. Sometimes these problems bring brothers and sisters together in an effort to cooperate, share the losses, and reevaluate the meaning of family, as they realize that now they are the survivors. The death of a parent may even markedly diminish competition between them because the parent, the prize over whose love the children battled even as adults, is no longer there to compete for.

But very often the death or disability of the parent serves only to deepen chasms that have developed between the siblings over the years, reactivating old rivalries, even those that have long been buried and supposedly forgotten, in the competition over who takes the hands-on responsibility for aging parents, who makes the decisions, and who is favored over the other when the estate is divided up.

•

Alan has made an irreconcilable break with his sister with whom he had maintained a contentious but ongoing relationship over the years. Both prickly people, Alan and Elaine have always been quick to put into words all of their hostilities and resentments—and there were many—toward one another as well as others. Nevertheless, they got together regularly on holidays a few times a year, talked on the telephone every few weeks, and made sure their children saw each other frequently enough to develop a sense of family.

Their mother's death, however, caused such contention and bitterness that they no longer speak. Because the sister had been their mother's main caretaker, especially during her last years, the will left her almost all of their parents' "heirlooms." Although they were of little monetary value and Alan had never shown an interest in them before, now he felt cheated. He demanded that the two siblings divide them up equally. Elaine refused and today they consider themselves enemies. "I don't need her and I don't want her. She's always been a pain in the neck," is the way he says he feels about it. Meanwhile, he thinks up new responses to her every day. She haunts him and he can't get her out of his mind.

The Older Years

In their later years, most people experience a powerful urge to turn back to their brothers and sisters, becoming much more involved and interested in them. Perhaps because siblings are the last links to the original family, the repositories of shared memories, the only lasting intimate connections, siblings become more valuable as the years go by, with elderly people feeling closer to their siblings than to any other relatives except their own children and perhaps their spouses.

Those siblings who have been close since childhood become even closer. And those who haven't are more willing to push aside their old feelings of resentment as they look to their siblings for support when the end of the road seems near. Sibling rivalry tends to diminish with age, as people usually become more understanding and tolerant of the differences between them. "If you don't have family now, who *do* you have?" asks a 75-year-old woman.

•

Lana, 66, spent her youth trying to get the attention of her brother Al, seven years her senior. Although there was another brother between them, Al was her sibling of significance, the one from whom she always sought recognition. "He ignored me, he was distant, he always thought he knew what was right and what was wrong, and he never hesitated to say so. Even after we were grown up and married with children, he was never interested in my career or what I thought about anything.

"He was very conservative politically, a real reactionary, a redneck in a way, and my weapon against him was to be just as outrageous as possible, voicing opinions far more radical than I actually felt and making snide remarks about his intense interest in money. I also made sure never to compliment him about anything and somehow I couldn't make it to his son's wedding. It's amazing when you think that he affected my whole life despite the fact that he left for college when I was in the fifth grade and never really came home again."

For many years, Lana and Al, who lived about a thousand miles apart, saw each other once a year at the most, then a couple of years would pass between visits. But two years ago, after their mother died, Al suffered a stroke and his sister felt a strong need to make peace with him before it was too late. "Because he was my brother, I could never have completely cut him off and now I felt it was our last chance to reconcile. Besides, after his stroke he was somehow reduced to human size in my eyes.

"I had never had a really good talk with him before in our lives," she relates. "Now for the first time we talked. We reminisced about growing up out in the country and I realized he had been a very unhappy boy who never felt he lived up to our parents' expectations. It was strange to hear that and wonderful too because it made him much more human and accessible to me. And even though we still disagreed about almost everything, I was able to push aside a lot of those old hostile feelings and finally accept him as a positive part of my life. That's given me a sense of peace that I never realized was missing."

•

This is a time when other sources of contact, support, and nurturance have dwindled, new friends are hard to make, and many people begin to feel alone in the world except for their families. In most cases, there's more time too to reminisce and worry about one another's health and well-being. Most important, older people are struck by the realization that their brothers and sisters aren't going to be around forever, and if they are going to try to become closer, they'd better do it now.

The sobering effect of confronting one's own mortality usually makes even nonbelievers wonder about life after death, and mending fences suddenly promises dividends with a possible payoff of eternal salvation. So this part of life is often driven by making peace and covering all bets.

Since you and your siblings are often the only remnants of your original family, in this phase of life you feel tremendous pressure to bury the old animosities and come to terms with the ones who are left. You are propelled toward each other by feelings of isolation, a need for affirmation of your own identity, a validation of your reminiscences, and a yearning for the family warmth you once experienced or always wanted. It's a time when most people want to make sense of their lives. Who better to help you do this than your siblings, who have known you longer than anyone?

Although adult children and spouses, when they are around, are usually your primary sources of support, you probably feel your siblings would be there for you if you needed them and that, in the event of a crisis, you would call on them for help and probably get it.

Men, in this stage of life as in others, generally tend to be shortchanged when it comes to having the ability to establish or reestablish closeness with their siblings and, in fact, often distance themselves even more than they may have before. Sisters may feel more competitive with one another but, at the same time, they are usually more in touch with their feelings, closer, more supportive, and more bonded. And, very important, they are the ones who usually assume the job of keeping all the siblings in touch and making sure everyone is all right. Even brothers, especially as they get older, often feel closest to a sister and are much more likely to stay in touch with her than with another brother.

The death of a brother or a sister is the last act, a tremendous assault on your sense of invincibility and immortality, forcing you to acknowledge that if this contemporary whom you expected to be there forever has gone, then your turn can't be far behind. Maybe, if your rivalry has raged on throughout the years, you have the perverse pleasure of outlasting your sibling in the race of life. But the loss makes you feel less protected and more alone, making closeness to the ones who are left even more important than ever before.

Damage Control:
Making Friends with Your Siblings

It's never too late to improve your relationship with a brother or sister. You may feel your connection with a sibling is good, but not quite all that you'd like it to be. You may feel it is operative but marred by resentments and loaded with leftover rivalries. Or maybe you consider it beyond repair, so remote, so rigid, or so hostile that there's no way it can ever be different. However, whatever its condition, almost any relationship can be changed if you are willing to put real energy into making it better.

Most of us want very much to be friends with our brother or sister. We yearn for a loving and devoted sibling whom we can trust, rely upon, respect, and a relationship filled with love and understanding where we are equals and free to be who we are without fear of rejection. We want those happy family get-togethers, replete with harmony, support and joy, instead of the unpleasant experiences they often turn out to be. We'd love to be freed from the unresolved rivalries of our childhoods, the jealousies, hurt feelings, rejections, or manipulations, and to be close to these people to whom we are irrevocably tied.

And if love and closeness are not in the cards, we'd like at least to be on good terms with them.

If you want your relationship with your siblings to be different, start making it happen. If it is essentially good, you can smooth the rough edges. If it is unhappy, you can almost always make surprising changes in it, even though you can't make yourself or your siblings over into new people. At best, your efforts to improve the relationship will result in new attitudes and behaviors on both of your parts and the beginnings of a new closeness. At the very least, you will have taken the edge off some of your own animosities by looking more objectively at yourself and your siblings, altering some of your attitudes, and doing your best to change a relationship that's been hampering you, perhaps even relentlessly darkening your view of the world, since you were a child. In making the effort to understand your brother or sister and reconcile your differences, you will experience a gain in personal growth because, no matter what happens, you will come away with important insights.

By taking responsibility for your own part in the competition and unhappiness between you, and making an effort to understand the roots of your siblings' feelings toward you, you will discover that both of you have been programmed by your own unique experiences to behave as you do and, in knowing that, you will be better able to accept them. That doesn't mean that you will end up loving a sibling you used to hate. You don't have to love him. You don't have to admire him. You don't even have to like him. But you have to accept him as he is, the product of his history, part of which is *you* and your effect on him. In the course of a lifetime, unless we are very special, we really don't affect many people's lives. Once you realize that your siblings are among the few, you may want to know them better so you can see the results of your influence and maybe take some pride, as a parent does, in what they have learned from you.

Remember that no relationship can ever be perfect, especially after a lifetime of rivalry, and if you demand perfection, you will never be satisfied. Be ready to settle for some improvement and continue to work toward more. No matter how many advances you make, you are both sure to retain the major hangups and pressure points you have developed over the years, and you will never turn into different people. You will never eliminate all of the tension between you. But even if your rivalry remains intense, it need not continue to be so overpowering that it casts a dark shadow over the rest of your life.

Be prepared to invest time and patience in making alterations. Nothing will change if you don't make an effort, especially if you haven't spoken to your sibling in years or you're poised for flight every time you hear that familiar voice on the telephone. Sometimes it even requires outside help. After all, both of you have spent a lifetime perfecting your attitudes and defensive behaviors. Change is not easy. The familiar is what we know. But you can do it if you examine the relationship with a real desire to make sense out of it.

True happiness can come from finally making peace with a sibling, particularly an SOS. When the mission is accomplished, it often proves to be the most extensive psychological movement that's possible to make within a lifetime. The connection between siblings is so profound that when you make changes in it, it carries with it major implications for every other area of your life. When you can finally deal with your sister, you will become better able to deal with the pseudo-sisters at work. When you make changes in your relationship with your brother, the diminished tension will surely rub off on your spouse and children. Positive change in one part of your life has to pay off in others.

How to Get Started

We have found from years of experience with our patients, almost all of whom have siblings and difficulties dealing with them, that there are many practical steps you can take to keep a good sibling relationship in working order and others that, in most cases, will help mend seriously frayed ties. All of them will help you stop running around in emotional circles and repeating the mistakes of the past.

But first, before you begin, there are some important points to remember:

• Although other families may appear to be in perfect harmony, they invariably have their own private problems and may, in fact, be in chaos. Don't waste your time envying them. Instead, get to work on the family you've got.

• Your siblings are not children anymore. They are adults who must be viewed and treated like adults. You will be tempted to see them as they once were, or as you once perceived them to be, but today they have many more dimensions and have moved far beyond being merely your little sister or your big brother.

• Making changes in a sibling relationship that doesn't measure up isn't going to happen all by itself. If you just go along as you always have, you'll perpetuate the status quo or let it deteriorate even more. You must deliberately work at it just as you would if your marriage were foundering.

• Remember that every family has its inequities. It's impossible for every sibling to have received the identical amount or intensity of parental love and attention, and one (or more) of you will resent perceived preferences. That is the nature of the sibling relationship and you can't escape it. Accept that as your starting point.

• Part of growing up is learning to appreciate the moment for what it is, to come to terms with what *is* and what *can* be. Don't expect too much. Presumably if you've gotten this far in this book you have learned that by its very nature the sibling relationship is a difficult one. Be happy with what you can get, savoring the benefits and letting go of the disappointments. Give what you can—which may never meet their expectations either—and expect from them, people with their own problems and agendas, only what they are capable of giving you at that particular moment.

• Don't let your pride—or stubbornness—persuade you that

your sibling must take the first step, even if you are certain he is in the wrong. You could wait forever, meantime allowing your resentment to become an unsupportable burden. Take the initiative. Make the overtures yourself, whether your purpose is to stay connected or to clear up misunderstandings. It doesn't mean you're a better person than your sibling because you've made the first move, nor does it mean that your job is now done and the rest is up to your brother or sister. You may have to persist.

• As adults, your siblings are who they are, the results of their own experience, composites of good and bad. They cannot *be* anybody else but the people they are, nor can they be transformed into dramatically different human beings. To them, reality is how they see a situation and how they respond to what they see. You may have spent a lifetime resenting them for their failure to be what you'd like them to be, but you can't change the past. *Stop hoping they will change.* Accept what they think as *their* reality. And how they feel about you as *their* truth. Instead of trying to make them over into people you *wish* they were and resenting them for their inadequacies, put your efforts into knowing them better, understanding their perspective, learning how they see you, and why they, like you, could not help behaving as they do. From their point of view, they are doing the best they can.

Realize, for example, that a youngest brother cannot respond to a challenge with the same natural confidence as an oldest brother. A middle sister who's felt lost in the crowd can't fully appreciate how another sibling, born first, feels entitled to lead the pack and take all the credit. A child who felt less loved, less respected, less able than his siblings can never totally forgive the others for his perceived deficiencies.

• You may find, after all your efforts to tighten the ties, that your brothers or sisters are not friendship material. But even then, you can come to some kind of understanding, realizing at last that they're not out to hurt you but, just like you, have merely been trying to survive. Given their experiences, their perspectives, their birth order, the labels and roles they were assigned by the family, their view of you as a competitor for a limited supply of love, they had no choice but to behave toward you as they did.

• Remember that maybe it wasn't easy growing up with *you* as competition. Perhaps your siblings had a tough time dealing with your determination to gain superiority over them and, in their eyes, your unrelenting efforts to get more than your fair share of love and attention. From the information you've gotten here, you can put on your siblings' shoes and go for a stroll. Walking in their shoes allows you to see that they had their own problems and are not all bad or all wrong.

• Lots of people—not just your siblings—have a stake in preserving your standard operating procedures just the way they are. As we have discussed earlier, they often want your relationship to be stable and recognizable. Your parents, other siblings, spouses, children, maybe even friends, may sense that if you and a sibling draw closer together, they will be pushed out and you may meet great resistance from them.

Parents frequently erect impenetrable barriers to reconciliation or exploration among their grown children for many reasons. Sometimes they fear pressure on themselves to change. Sometimes they don't want their failings as parents to be exposed. Often they feel they have much to protect, such as the attention on themselves, by keeping their offspring in competition with or estranged from one another. In seriously dysfunctional families, the parents may have a huge investment in making the siblings continue to perform according to their familiar scripts.

So they erect roadblocks that their children are afraid to breach. That's why we have often found that sibling relationships improve dramatically after their parents' deaths. When parents are no longer around to represent the elusive prize that each sibling so badly wants to win, the competition may diminish. As one woman said, "We were really competing for Mom's love. Each of us wanted to be the one she really depended on, the one she was closest to, the one she loved best. Since she was impossible to please, we each felt the other one must have gotten it all. When she was gone, the tension diminished and we could finally relax and enjoy one another."

Spouses and other siblings, too, often play a large part in preventing brothers and sisters from making peace because they have an investment in the estrangement or because they are jealous of the closeness. A husband may want to keep his wife exclusively to himself without interference from a family member. A wife may resent a sibling's influence on her husband. A sibling may fear being left out of the equation when two other siblings make friends.

Maintaining a Good Sibling Relationship

First, let's talk about how to keep a functional sibling relationship, one that has its glitches and disappointments but is essentially healthy, in good working order. All sibling relationships, even the best of them, are vulnerable and easily damaged, and so they require attention and an ongoing maintenance program to keep them running smoothly. If you devote some energy to them, you'll find it pays off by helping you avoid misunderstandings and strengthen family ties. Later, we'll discuss the most effective way we have found to mend sibling ties that are in need of extensive repair.

To maintain a good relationship with your brother or sister, keep the following "rules" in mind:

• Always clear the air as quickly as possible when there are conflicts or injured feelings, major or minor. Resentments and misunderstandings will only grow more intense if you are afraid to confront them, so talk about them as soon as they occur. If you can't do it immediately, force yourself to find an opportunity to talk a little later. Simply say, "I need to talk to you about this because it's been bothering me." And then state your views, being very careful not to resort to accusations or open hostility.

•

"I go around thinking she and I get along so well and yet she always manages to say something that upsets me," says Katherine, speaking of her sister Sue. "Like recently I told her Jim and I were going on a biking vacation in England. Her response was, 'Aren't you too old for that kind of thing?' It was like we were two kids again and I was made to feel stupid and uncertain once more. Why did she say that? I want to be good friends with her but sometimes it's very hard."

Katherine could have advanced her relationship with her sister, rather than slink away feeling hurt and resentful, if she had had the courage to ask for an explanation immediately. A calm, "I don't understand why you said that. What do you mean?" may well have resulted in better understanding between them. She may have learned, for example, that her affinity for adventure made Sue feel inadequate compared to her; that Sue, still feeling protective of her little sister, was concerned for her safety; or that, burdened by a chronically ill husband, she was envious of her sister's good times.

The short-term peacekeeping effect of ignoring a conflict or a disappointment between you and your sibling can't work out to your benefit in the long run because it buries the issues once more and pushes you farther apart. Leaving bad feelings unattended creates distance between you and prevents real intimacy. Walking around minor irritations is fine, if you do it consciously, and so is agreeing to disagree on touchy subjects. And sometimes, problems get solved by doing nothing at all but letting them simmer for a while. But once resentments have begun to build up, the damage becomes more difficult to repair and the relationship enters the realm of "tit for tat"—"You did this to me so I'll retaliate by doing that to you"—a scenario that's difficult to quit.

• When your brother or sister speaks, *listen*. What he or she is saying is important and you must take it seriously even if you have heard it dozens of times before. In fact, when you *have* heard it many times before, it means he thinks you didn't get the message. And that is probably the correct interpretation. Don't tune out.

• Respect the boundaries of your relationship, the parameters beyond which it is unwise to encroach. These parameters change over time and should be recognized if peace and good will are to prevail. When you were children, you may have shared all your thoughts and feelings, but in later life, your primary loyalties may now be focused on other people, such as your spouse, and there are secrets to be kept. So accept the fact that you may have to keep your distance in some respects and that your sibling, too, may not feel free to share the most intimate details of his life or his decision-making process with you at all times.

• Don't make the assumption that it's your brother or sister who is always wrong when there are misunderstandings between you. We all want to look like fine people and feel it reflects negatively on us when we don't get along well with our brothers or sisters, so we usually put the blame on them, just as divorced people do with their ex-spouses. But they are not always at fault, or at least not completely at fault. You have probably played a part in producing this uncomfortable situation too. So be willing to listen, seriously consider his point of view, and acknowledge your own part in the affair. Don't hesitate to explain statements or actions you feel were misinterpreted, but be sure to tell him you are sorry for the confusion, admit your own failings, and recognize *in words* how he is feeling. Say, for example, "You must have felt really angry and now I understand why."

• Show up. Every family has its own expectations of its members and you should try to fulfill them if they are not unreasonable. Most families, for example, expect you to make a real attempt to attend their functions if that is reasonably possible, interpreting nonappearances as signs of lack of interest or even hostility.

When Bob's brother Jonathan, for example, didn't come to the baptism of his baby, Bob said nothing to him about it, but he told us, when Jonathan's daughter was born, "I made damn sure I didn't get there for her christening."

•

Charlotte is a woman of 56 who has maintained a close and supportive connection with her sister and brother-in-law despite the usual disappointments in the relationship. "If you're invited to an important family occasion," she advises, "you've got to show up! If you don't, you have signaled that you don't care enough to bother. I live over a hundred miles from my sister and she's having a graduation party for her daughter next week. Now you have to believe I don't feel like driving down there on a Saturday night in the summer. I have other things on my agenda. But I am going. Why? Because it's very important to her and I want to stay on good terms with my sister."

You may not always feel like going to your spouse's or children's events, but you do. Do the same for your siblings. The same kind of maintenance applies to birthdays, anniversaries, and other noteworthy occasions. Train yourself to remember them with a card, a gift, or a call, if not with a visit.

• Don't wait for your siblings to make all the contacts. A sibling who feels he has to pursue you feels rejected, punished, and resentful. How often have we heard, "He never calls me. I have to call him, and then he's late for his golf game or he's watching his favorite television program." Making the first move with your siblings, at least part of the time, shows that you acknowledge their existence and are interested in them. Besides, it eliminates the need for excuses and maneuvers.

• Be there when you are needed. Nothing draws people closer together than seeing one another through hard times. As so many of us say, "If you can't count on family, who *can* you count on?" We all feel better when we can share our burdens with others, and if we cannot turn to a brother or sister, we have greatly reduced our reserves for getting through crises.

• Use your reminiscences as a nonthreatening, nonconfrontive way to communicate with your siblings. Piecing together the past and recalling non-loaded events from your childhood give you an indirect way of dealing with tensions between you. It reestablishes intimacy and reaffirms your bonds, reminding you that only you two have such an emotional investment in these memories. It helps to cement the connection between you.

Most siblings reminisce about old times without planning ahead, but you can deliberately use your nonthreatening recollections as a tool to help you get closer to your brother or sister. You can begin by saying, "The other day I started thinking about the time . . ."

Or make a family photo album. Call all your siblings and collect as many old pictures of yourselves as you can. When everyone is together, maybe at holiday time, spend an hour assembling the book. Then have copies made for everybody to keep and pass on to their children later.

• Make time to be together. Surely you make plans to go away for the weekend with friends. Occasionally you have dinner with your colleagues, or spend a leisurely Sunday picnicking in the park with the neighbors. It is even more important to fit your brothers or sisters into your busy schedule because intimate relationships require time to share thoughts and develop trust.

• Most important of all: Let your brothers or sisters know you care about them. Coming right out and saying "You know, I really love you," or "I think about you so often and I want to tell you how much you mean to me" doesn't come easy for most of us except in the context of a romantic or parent-child relationship. But the real affection you feel for a sibling should not go unexpressed. If you can't bring yourself to say such things face to face or even on the telephone, write a note. Perhaps you fear rejection or a response like, "Well, you don't show it!" But if you mean it, your expression of caring can heal many wounds.

Everyone wants to be loved and appreciated, especially by those whose opinions matter the most. So show your affection, too, with a hug, a kiss, a compliment that you really mean, an unexpected gift, an invitation, a phone call, a note, a card. Don't wait for times of trouble or celebration, such as an illness or a wedding, but express your love and interest whenever you can do it with sincerity. And don't forget, too, to show your appreciation for gestures sent your way.

Repairing Serious Rifts

Sometimes the chasm between you and a sibling has become so wide and deep that it requires much more than everyday maintenance and minor repairs. Sometimes it needs to be shaken up and pieced back together. Using our experience as therapists, we are going to lead you through some steps our patients have found helpful in reconciling differences with siblings with whom they have come to a serious impasse.

First, Thoughts on Therapy

We believe that the very best route to a lasting peace with your siblings is to understand the power you have over one another. And one of the most effective ways to go about that is to go into therapy, either on your own or, even better, as a family, although we realize you may not feel psychologically ready for this—most people consider therapy only when their worlds are falling apart—or may not have the money, the time, the faith, or the energy required.

However, it is our contention that therapy is the quickest and most effective way to understand what's been going on all these years. Having a trained person present to guide you, whether you go to a professional therapist alone or together, can make a tremendous difference in discovering where each of you is coming from. With help, you are freer to express your innermost feelings because the therapist is there to keep everything under control, ask pertinent questions, provide direction, make interpretations. Therapy need not be a long-term commitment and, in fact, it usually requires only a few sessions to start making some important alterations in your relationship. These sessions can give you sufficient insight to continue your progress without professional assistance. It can help give you the jump-start that you and your relationship need.

We all have feelings, yet it never fails to astonish us that so many people are unable to identify them, probably because admitting to "ugly" or "unacceptable" emotions signifies to them that they are bad people. Often we have to *suggest* to our patients what their emotions may possibly be and give them "permission" to experience them before they can admit to them. In other words, by letting them know that all human beings have these same "unacceptable" feelings, we help our patients deal with them on a conscious and constructive level.

If seeing a therapist is out of the question for you, it is quite possible, though not nearly as easy, to make changes on your own. But remember, if you find yourself over your head in your efforts to improve your relationship with a sibling, getting the help of an experienced, licensed counselor may be the prudent way to go.

Getting Going on Your Own

Start by taking an inventory of the problems between you and your brother or sister. Ask yourself where you fit in your family in terms of labels, role, birth order, and how you typically behave, especially when you are on the defensive. With the help of our discussions, try to face your feelings of competition, hostility, guilt, inferiority, envy, and try to imagine what your brother or sister feels about you. One useful way to help identify your hidden emotions is to make a list of every possible feeling, positive and negative, and then to use it as a checklist. Another is to use the critical-event method, which we will describe later.

Now, let's assume you have decided to make a serious move toward establishing a friendship or at least an accord with your sibling. Contact him or her and say you'd like to talk. If you've had a stormy relationship or have cut yourself off from your brother or sister, this may represent an act of great courage.

Keep in mind that, although the time has come for trying to repair the unsatisfying bond with your sibling, he or she may not be ready for your overtures. So you must be patient and, as we will discuss, wait for the right opportunity. Your brothers or sisters may not feel the same urgency or have the same need to change. They may not be all that willing to deal with the issues that you consider so important or to have you back in their lives at the same moment or with the same intensity you'd like to have them back in yours.

When you talk, you must be willing to share your honest feelings. Many of us hesitate to reveal ourselves to our lifelong rivals, fearing that our feelings of envy, jealousy, inferiority, frustration, anger, or guilt will be interpreted as childish or neurotic, or brushed off as unimportant. But until these emotions are brought out into the open, there's no chance of improving the relationship. So, even if your overtures are met with "Don't be ridiculous! How could you feel like that?" or "You're getting hysterical, as usual," hang in there and let it be known that this is how you truly feel and you're trying to be as honest as you can: "Maybe I am getting hysterical because you aren't listening to what I'm saying!" In return, accept your sibling's feelings with respect without denying or denigrating them.

Don't be afraid of anger, an argument, even a major battle. You have undoubtedly repressed your feelings to the point where perhaps the only way you can express them is in anger, indignation, or despair. So what? That's communication, maybe the first really penetrating communication between you in years. Being open and truthful, especially when it evokes a revealing response, is the only way to make real progress. An honest explosion is better than a continuation of the resentment or repression of your feelings. You must lay your feelings out on the table *and* allow your sibling to do the same. That means giving each other all the time you need, without interruption.

Never leave this conversation open-ended. Speaking out truthfully is essential but only the beginning and storming out in anger or frustration stops the process cold. The next step is to talk positively about making changes that will improve the relationship. If you reach no understanding the first time around, go back and re-open the lines of communication for reclarification and negotiation.

How to Get Started

If your relationship with a sibling has been poor for many years or has suffered a serious rift, don't think you can change it in a day. Just do something to get things rolling. Pick up the telephone and say, "Hey, listen, you know what? I've been reading a book about sibling relationships and it made me think about us. Could we get together and talk? I really need your help in understanding some of my own problems, so let's set a time and a place, O.K.?" Or, "I love you but I hate the way we get sometimes when we're together. If we talked, I'm sure we could work it out."

Many of our patients have said they'd prefer confronting their siblings in a letter or on the telephone, but we object to both these means of communication unless there is no other way. Go ahead and write a letter spelling out your grievances and misunderstandings with your brother or sister—but don't send it. Read it over and then tear it up. Letters are a dangerous method of communication because they are so easily misinterpreted.

Telephone calls are tricky because this may be a volatile interaction and it's much too easy for one of you to hang up in a huff. Although calls may be the only way to go when personal visits aren't possible, they do not provide the optimal setting for resolving differences or talking out feelings.

On the other hand, calls and letters can be used to make subtle advances on the road to changing the way things are. A birthday call, a call to chat for no reason at all, an offer of help when things are not right, a reminiscence about a happy time together, a note showing concern and interest in your sibling's life, can help to get the relationship started on a more satisfying track.

What you must do, if it is in any way possible to arrange, is to talk about your relationship in person because this is the most effective way to break through the barriers between you. It gives you the opportunity to look in one another's face and experience the intensity of the feelings. And it allows the time to hear one another out and talk the situation over.

Using the Critical Event

Now, before you get together, you have important preparation to do. You and your sibling, just like a husband and wife or parent and child, have shared a number of "critical events" that carry enormous emotional baggage along with them. These critical events are incidents, major or minor, that have stayed with you over the years, incidents that you have never forgotten. Why? Because they are representative of the way you see the relationship between you. Much like the early recollections and dreams typically used by psychoanalysts as tools to get inside a patient and share his view of the world, these events can be extremely helpful in getting to your real feelings.

Stop reading for a moment and think about your brother or sister. What incident sticks in your mind the most? What you recall may seem as insignificant as a look of elation on your sister's face when you failed a spelling test in the second grade or as important as a bloody fistfight between you when you were ten. It could be the time your sister comforted you when you broke your favorite doll. Or the day you both went to a party and you stole your brother's girl. Whatever critical event you recall, it stands out among all others in your mind because it symbolizes your view of the relationship between you. There may be one, or a number, of events. They tell a very important story.

•

One of our patients, Jeanne, a woman in her 50s, remembered an event that occurred when she was a skinny little girl of 8. Their mother had asked her older sister Rosalie, then 13, to take her downtown to the dentist that afternoon after school. Rosalie, protesting vociferously at the injustice of the task, grabbed Jeanne by the hand, yanked her down the street, across avenues and over bridges, never loosening her tight grip despite tearful protests and mighty struggles, all the way to the dentist—and back. To the younger sister, this incident symbolized how controlling she felt Rosalie had always been.

•

Such moments are composite pictures of how you see your relationship with a brother or sister. They sum up scores of similar moments and are related to hundreds of variations on the same theme. As such, they provide quick access to your inner feelings.

A critical event that symbolizes your relationship is what you must discuss with your brother or sister, rather than bringing up an amorphous generalized feeling such as "You were always bossing me around" or "You made me feel like I was stupid."

First, spend some time thinking about your sister or brother. What is the event that comes to mind? Write it down on paper in detail. What happened? Where did it happen? How old were you? What were you wearing? What did you look like? Who said what? Who did what? Who else was present? What did they do? What did it mean to you? What is it saying about you and your sibling? Why have you held on to this memory? Decide how you felt *then* about that event and how you feel about it *now*. Did you feel anger, humiliation, frustration, glee, power, powerlessness, triumph, envy, guilt? List all of your feelings, then and now, about what happened and ask yourself if it still represents a problem between you. In Jeanne's case, she saw herself as her sister's victim, belittled, humiliated, and overpowered, just as she does to this day despite the passage of time.

The next question to ask yourself is: What was the problem that is represented by this incident? In Jeanne's case, the problem was feeling belittled, humiliated, and overpowered. In your story, what was your feeling and does it still represent a problem between you?

•

When Lynn was asked to recall a critical event from her child-hood, she promptly came up with a symbolic scene between herself and her sister, who was four years older. She saw herself sitting on her big sister's bed and rubbing her back. That was it, no more and no less. Then, when she was asked about her feelings at the time, she remembered feeling warm and friendly. Why was she rubbing her sister's back? To make her feel better, to comfort her after another fight with Dad.

"Julie could get me to do anything if she made me feel sorry for her because, while I envied her for being the center of attention, she was always in trouble and that made me feel bad even though she usually acted as if I didn't exist. It always made me feel good if I could make her feel better. Later, when we grew up, she got married and pretty much ignored me for years until her husband died and she was all alone. She started making overtures and I was ready to take care of her again, "rub her back," so to speak, although I was angry, too, that I'd been discarded when I wasn't needed. And I guess that's the way it still is."

The recollection served to sum up Lynn's perspective on her relationship with her sister. She eventually understood that, un-less she stopped playing the role of nursemaid/caretaker and de-veloped other ways of interacting with Julie, she would surely find herself superfluous again when her help was no longer needed.

All this from a little piece of a memory, an entire set of feelings stored up in a seemingly innocent sliver of information.

Looking at the Other Side

Now think about your brother or sister. How do you think he or she was feeling during that event?

Jeanne, whose sister yanked her down the street by the hand to the dentist's office, decided that her older sister must have felt she was a burden, a pain-in-the-neck kid whom she didn't like in the first place and who came along when she was five and stole away her mother's love. "I was the favorite child in our family, I always knew that, and my sister must have resented that terribly.

She must have been very jealous because she was 'the difficult one' and I was 'the good girl,' always trying to please my mother. She'd probably have much rather thrown me in front of a car than take responsibility for my welfare. Besides, she surely had better things to do that day. To her I was an ungrateful rebellious brat who was dumped on her and didn't appreciate what she had to do for me. I can't believe it! After all those years of resentment, now *I'm* feeling sorry for *her*!"

•

For a more objective reading, discuss the incident you have recalled from your past with a few friends or colleagues. To keep yourself honest, be sure at least one of them had your sibling's birth-order position. Ask for their opinion of what you and your sibling were feeling and attempting to achieve at the time. Because people who grew up in the same birth order position have experienced similar kinds of events and feelings, they may shed some light on what your sibling was experiencing, helping you to empathize with the other side of the story.

Now get ready for one of the most emotionally draining conversations you'll ever have. Be prepared to admit you could be wrong and don't assume that your sibling is the party solely responsible for any of the problems the two of you have with each other. If you go into this exercise taking the position that the other person is no damn good and has no positive feelings for you, nothing constructive can possibly occur. Attitude is all-important because persistent rancor blocks insights. Remember, there are indeed two sides to every story.

However, you are not to blame for everything that has gone wrong between you, either. You bring only fifty percent of the responsibility to the relationship. The point is to get beyond blame and start the repair work.

Timing your opening conversation with a sibling may not be easy. You must be patient and wait for the moment when your brother or sister seems open to a discussion of times past. Take a chance when feelings are running high and close to the surface, perhaps during a family crisis that stirs the emotions, such as the illness or death of a parent, or a special happening such as a marriage, the birth of a child, economic stress, divorce.

But don't take advantage of your sibling when he's down or so overstressed with work, obligations, or emotions that he doesn't have the time or the energy for a productive conversation. And don't choose Thanksgiving dinner at the family homestead for a heavy discussion. You don't want to cause a scene, nor should you be distracted or interrupted by other people who may have their own agendas. You need to talk privately.

When you feel the time is right, tell your brother or sister, in person or, if there's no other choice, on the telephone, that you've been doing a lot of soul-searching about your relationship and you'd like to share your thoughts. Ask if he or she would be open to it.

Of course, if your sibling says, "No, I don't want to talk about anything. Forget it. There's nothing to discuss. What's the point of rehashing all this? It's water under the bridge," and means it, then you have no option. You'll have no engagement with him and no improvement in your relationship. If your sibling refuses to participate, you may as well find that out in the beginning, although we suggest that you try—again and again—because maybe the timing or your approach was not propitious. But in most cases, your siblings will be intrigued and interested simply because they, too, crave the warmth and caring of a good relationship. They, too, would love to leave the resentments behind and make friends with you.

Sometimes, of course, the relationship has become so damaged over the years that it is beyond repair. In that case, we counsel our patients to walk away and keep their distance, replacing those sibling ties with other close relationships. This is the healthiest choice under the circumstances.

No Emotion, No Progress

When you get together, state that you are there to listen and you hope that he or she is willing to listen to you, too. Try to keep the conversation centered on the critical event you have remembered. You might introduce it by saying, "This is something that happened between us that's bothered me all my life. I'd really like to find out your feelings about it." Then describe the incident. With that bait, the other person should respond because for him, too, this conversation is loaded with emotional baggage.

Your brother or sister will have total recall of the critical event, remembering it in complete detail although from another point of view. Try to stick exclusively with the incident without going off into "You always hated me!" and be sure to allow each of you plenty of time to tell your side of the story without interruption. If your sibling doesn't remember the event, choose another or ask him if it seems likely to have happened. If he denies it was likely, then ask how he thinks the scene would have played out if it did happen. That way you have gotten him to commit to a perspective of how things were, allowing you to go on to the next phase.

The more conflict now the better, from our point of view. The power that these incidents evoke can be frightening, sometimes turning gentle souls into fire-eating beasts, and your tendency may be to run away from it. But force yourself to stay with it, tearing apart the single incident. The conflict that comes from this intense discussion will in the long run improve your sibling bond immensely.

What is essential here is involvement, anger, honesty, emotion. No productive interchange is possible unless you are both thoroughly engaged in the confrontation. If you are angry and upset and your sibling remains calm, aloof, and controlled, you can be sure he or she is working very hard to maintain the status quo. You must break through that calm to move on to new territory. Nor can you allow your sibling to put you off by resorting to tears, panic attacks, hysterics.

At the same time, if you find that you are resorting to your old tried-and-true defensive techniques such as guilting or rejection, recognize them as a warning sign that the issues under discussion are especially heavily loaded. Back off and present your feelings in a less threatening manner.

If the situation becomes overcharged or out of control, you may have to deescalate. Suggest you stop talking for a while to evaluate what's happened: "Maybe we should talk about this later. I'll come back tomorrow." Or, switch to a less emotionally charged subject and give yourselves the chance to relax.

Remember to Listen

It is most important to remember that you must *listen*. Listen carefully to what your sibling is telling you because it will always have some validity and much of what this person is saying about you and your behavior may well be true. In any case, it is true from his or her perspective. Take it seriously.

You will find that once the two of you have reached this stage, you can't leave it alone. You have both invested in the issues and you won't be able to drop them until the air has been cleared. Although you may become extremely agitated and the hostile words may fly, it is very doubtful that no progress in understanding will be made. In fact, anger is the signal that the other person has become seriously involved. That's when new patterns will emerge because, open with your sibling at last, you are finally saying exactly what you mean. When that happens, the relationship is going to move forward. Guaranteed.

Suppose your brother or sister stands up and says, "This is a broken record. I've heard all this before!" You can respond, "Maybe, but let's not stop here. Let's keep going and maybe we'll finally understand one another. Please, tell me more about how you feel and I'll do my best to be honest with you. Then we'll make some sense out of it."

Whatever happens, *never* walk away and *never* drop it there. Reopen communications immediately, perhaps the next day. Then don't go back with anger, and don't lay blame or guilt on the other person, or all is lost. Be sure to give credence to his perspective. Most people are happy to continue a conversation when they think their sibling is beginning to see their side of the story. Now is the time to renegotiate. Let your brother or sister know you've thought about what has been said and now have some understanding of his or her point of view. Be openly empathetic. Say something like, "I've been thinking about what you said and I've decided you are right about a lot of things. Tell me more about how you feel."

Or if the situation calls for it, even forty years after the fact, make an apology for behavior your sibling found unsupportable: "I'm really sorry I stole your girl in high school. I always felt inferior to you. You were so good at everything. And I guess I did it to get even with you and prove there was one area where you weren't always better than me. Please accept my apology now. I've felt very guilty about it but never dared bring it up. I had hoped you'd forgotten."

And don't forget to add, if this is how you truly feel, "You know, I have always loved you and I want to be your friend."

Then, "Let's talk some more because it has helped me tremendously. When can we get together again?" It may take months before your brother or sister is willing to continue the discussion, but he or she has heard you and has had to think about what you've both said.

And even if your sibling refuses to extend the negotiations, don't feel you have failed. You have been courageous and resourceful. Often when we plant seeds, it takes months for them to sprout. You may well have succeeded in producing new perspectives for both of you and, at the very least, your actions have given you plenty to think about. Let a little time go by and try again.

•

Remember that the rewards of establishing closer relationships with the only brothers or sisters you're ever going to have can be enormously gratifying. Work at them, strengthen them, make the most of them, and you will surely profit. If we have accomplished anything in this book, we hope it is to encourage you to look closely at your siblings, recognize their powerful influence on you, see their permanent place in your life, and view them as people with problems and agendas that are different from yours. And, finally, to accept the good and the bad in them, human beings who are doing the best they can.

Your efforts may fail to result in the friendship and closeness you are yearning for, but they will certainly improve the quality of your life because now you have a better understanding of the past. You have learned to see your siblings and yourself with more generosity.

And if your efforts do bring you closer, you have both come out winners.

•

In the meantime, your examination of your family has surely helped you achieve an even more important goal—and that is to understand yourself more clearly. Because your siblings were such a potent force in shaping your personality and determining your future, you can't even begin to know yourself without first comprehending your relationship with them.

You have learned that the sibling relationship is, in its way, the most powerful relationship you will ever have because it established the roots of rivalry. It is even more powerful in its way than that with your parents because the way you learned to interact with your brothers or sisters set the pattern for how you will behave in all of your relationships for the rest of your life. Growing up in fierce competition for love, approval, and attention, you and your siblings will never stop trying to come out looking better than the other, always wanting to be the child Mommy loved best, the one Daddy admired most. Sibling rivalry is normal, natural, and universal, an inescapable ingredient of the Sibling Complex.

You've learned too that you occupy a unique space in your family based on many factors that include birth order, gender, favoritism, the family's economic and emotional status, the size of the family. That you acquired labels the moment you were born, maybe even before, and have developed a role that you can now perform by remote control and a style of behavior that you take with you wherever you go.

It has taken courage to examine the Sibling Complex, the pervasive effects of the *other* most important relationship in your life, still one of the biggest blind spots in our culture. But by letting some light shine on it, you have surely gained a deeper understanding of yourself and your siblings. And perhaps you have grown closer to your brothers or sisters, or at least more tolerant of their flaws and admiring of their strengths, as well as your own.